THIS BOOK BELONGS TO:

_____

_____

_____

HOW TO USE THIS BOOK:

In a reverse coloring book, you get to explore your artistic side by filling in the blank spaces of an already colored canvas. Complete your work of art by drawing lines, shapes, patterns, and various forms in the white and colored areas of the pages.

The beautiful thing about reverse coloring books is that they are therapeutic. As you go through the process of drawing, filling in the shapes and outlines, you also work on alleviating your stress and anxiety. Who wouldn't want that?

Welcome to your new coloring book in reverse! Take some time to explore a book that offers you a pleasurable and soothing coloring experience.

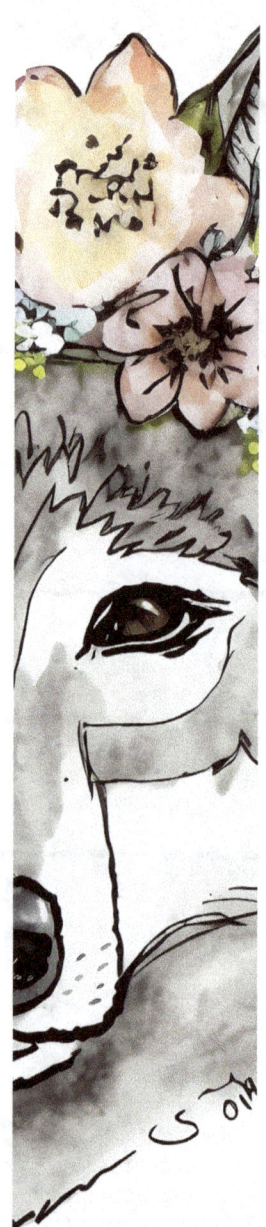

TIPS:

Choose your coloring supplies: You can color with black or any dark-colored pencils, markers, pens, or whatever else you like, as long as they won't bleed through the pages, that is.

Choose the first page: Flip through the book to choose your first page. You can browse the book from cover to cover or go around to different pages. You decide where you want to start.

Begin coloring: Fill in the blank areas surrounding the colored outlines first. Use multiple colors to achieve a more complicated appearance or use one color to make patterns. Just have fun.

Take pauses: Coloring can be calming, but to avoid eye and hand strain, it's vital to take intervals and stretch. Also, you can use this time to consider your coloring routine and show gratitude for your completed coloring pages.

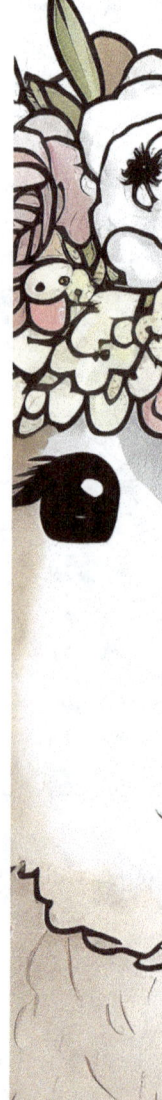

INFINITE POTENTIAL FOR CUSTOMISATION AND CREATIVITY:

There are countless opportunities for creativity and customization with this reverse coloring book. You can experiment with various color schemes, alter the pre-colored outlines, merge colors for a 3D appearance, add patterns and textures, and use various coloring techniques to produce one-of-a-kind and lovely drawings, regardless of your level of coloring expertise.

REVERSE COLORING IDEAS:

Try some of these to get you started.

Stacking Shapes
Dots
Waves
Stacked Lines
Thick Lines
Loopty-loops
Spirals
Little Shapes
Repeating Patterns
Hearts and Stars

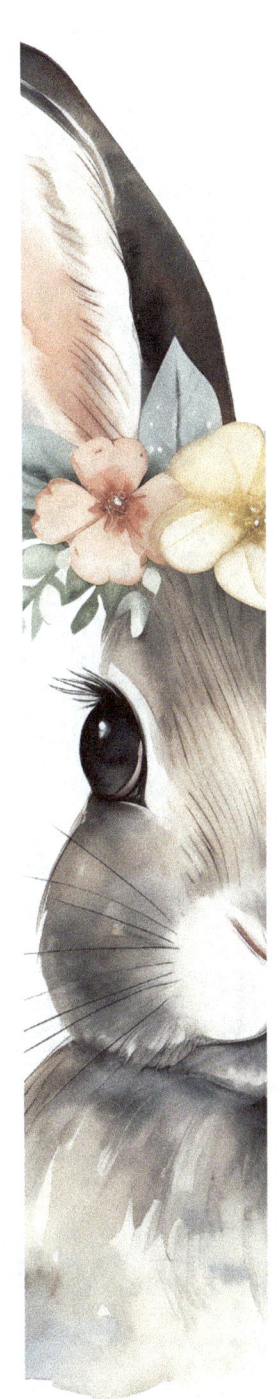

SOME PATTERNS TO GET YOU STARTED:

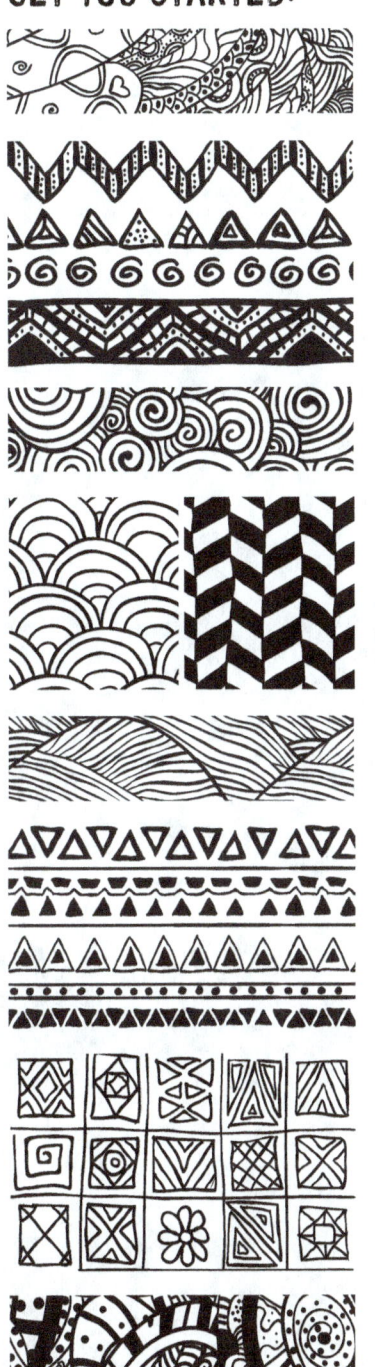

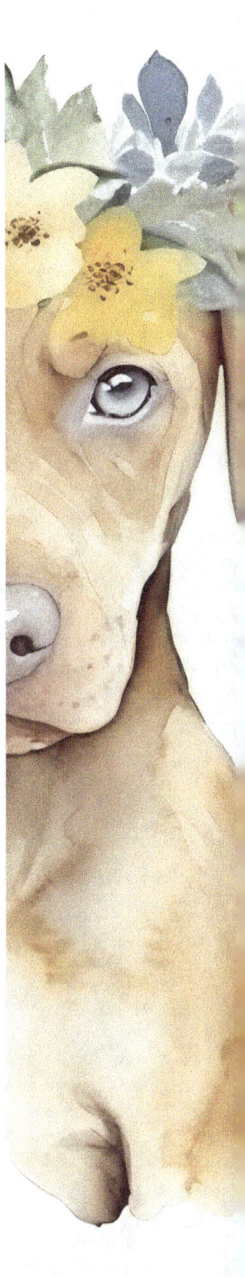

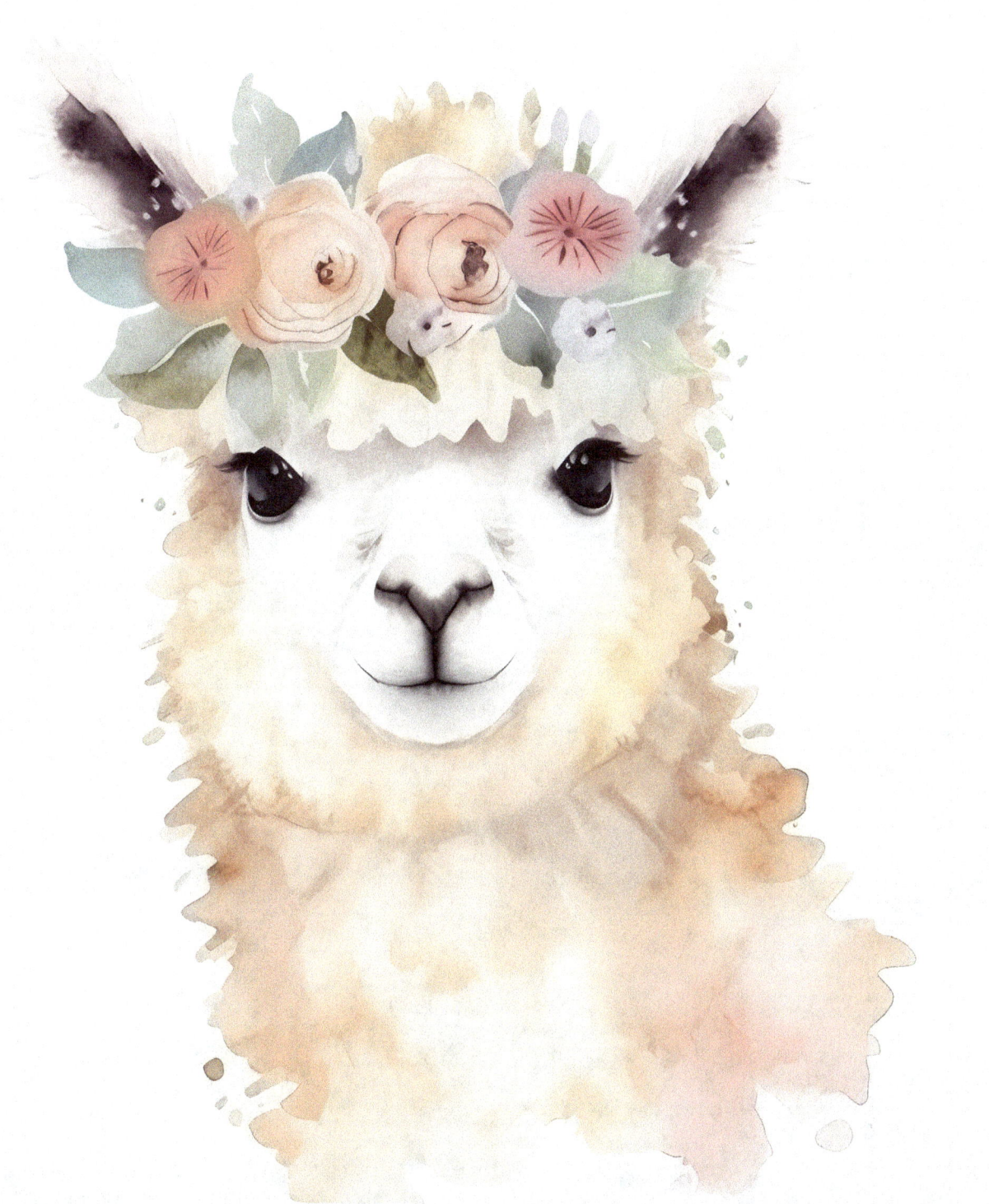

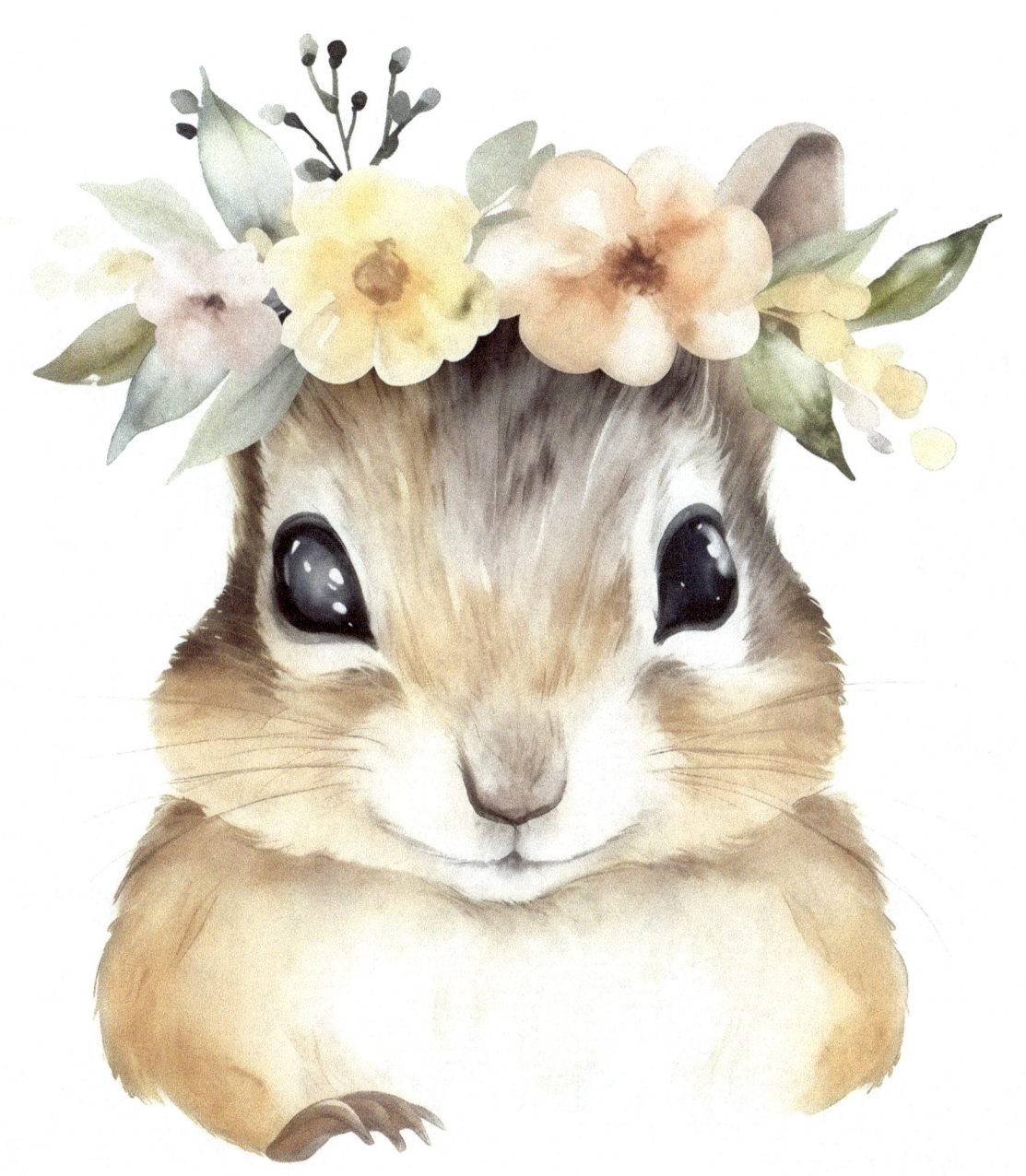

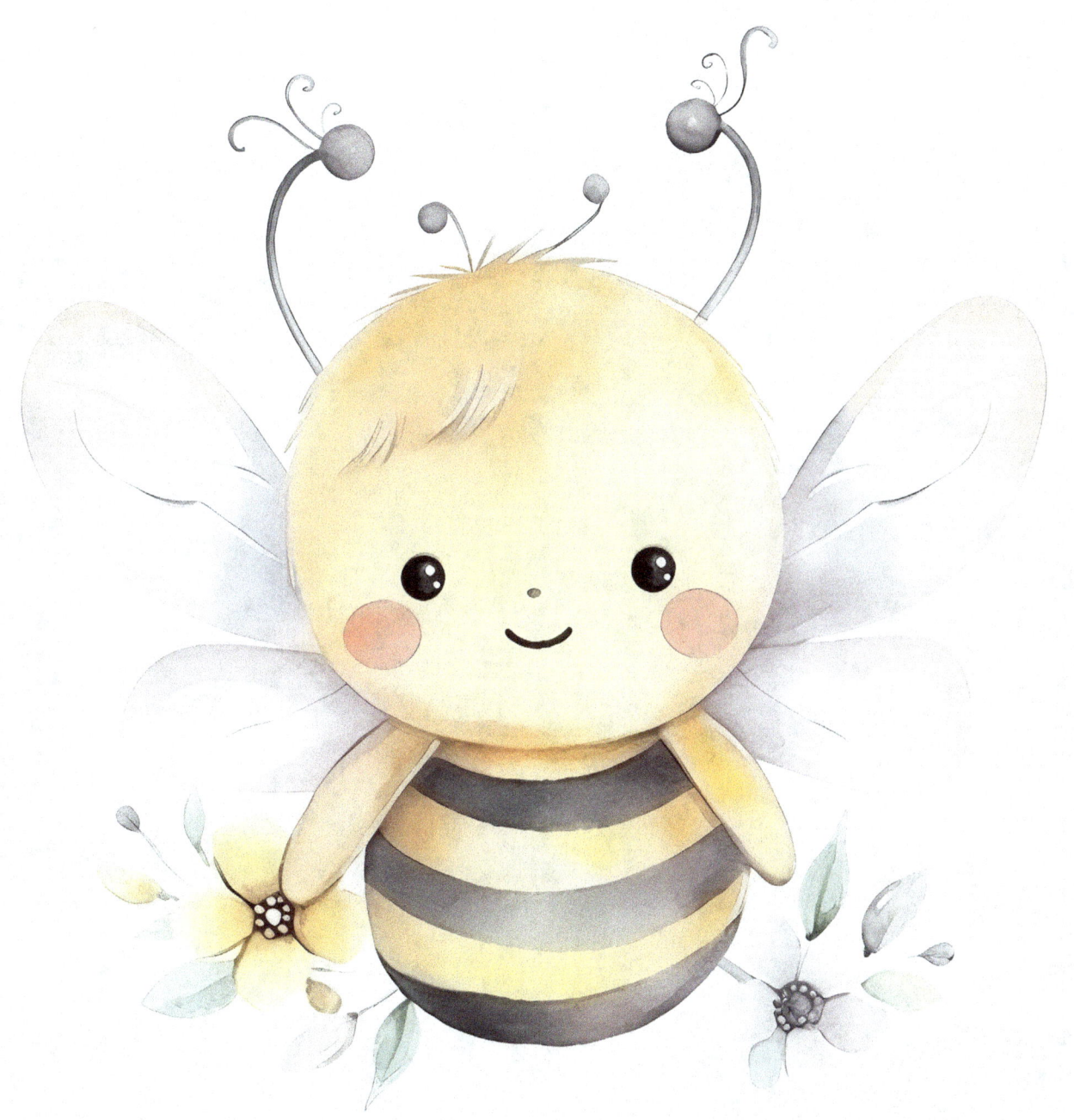

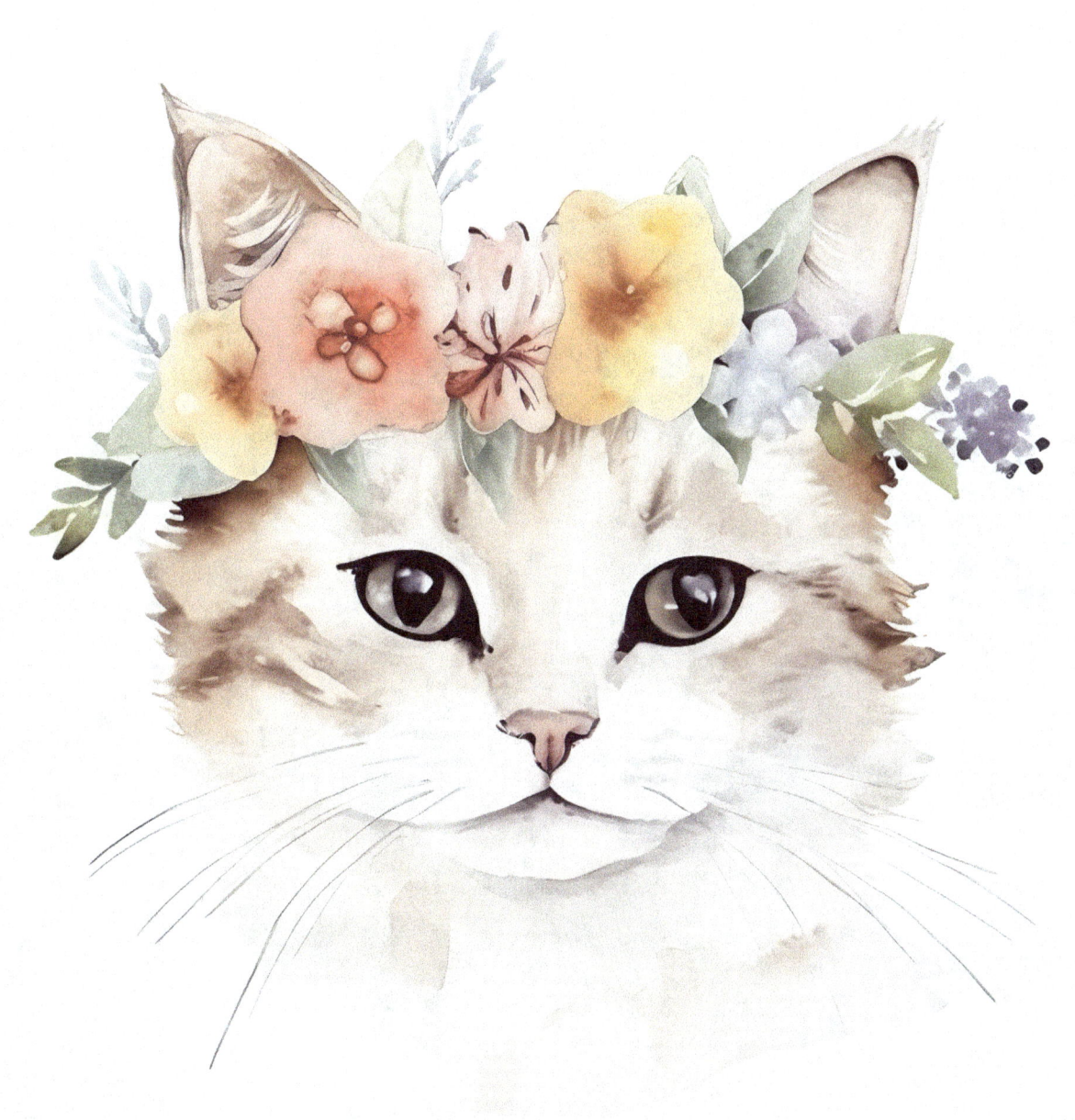

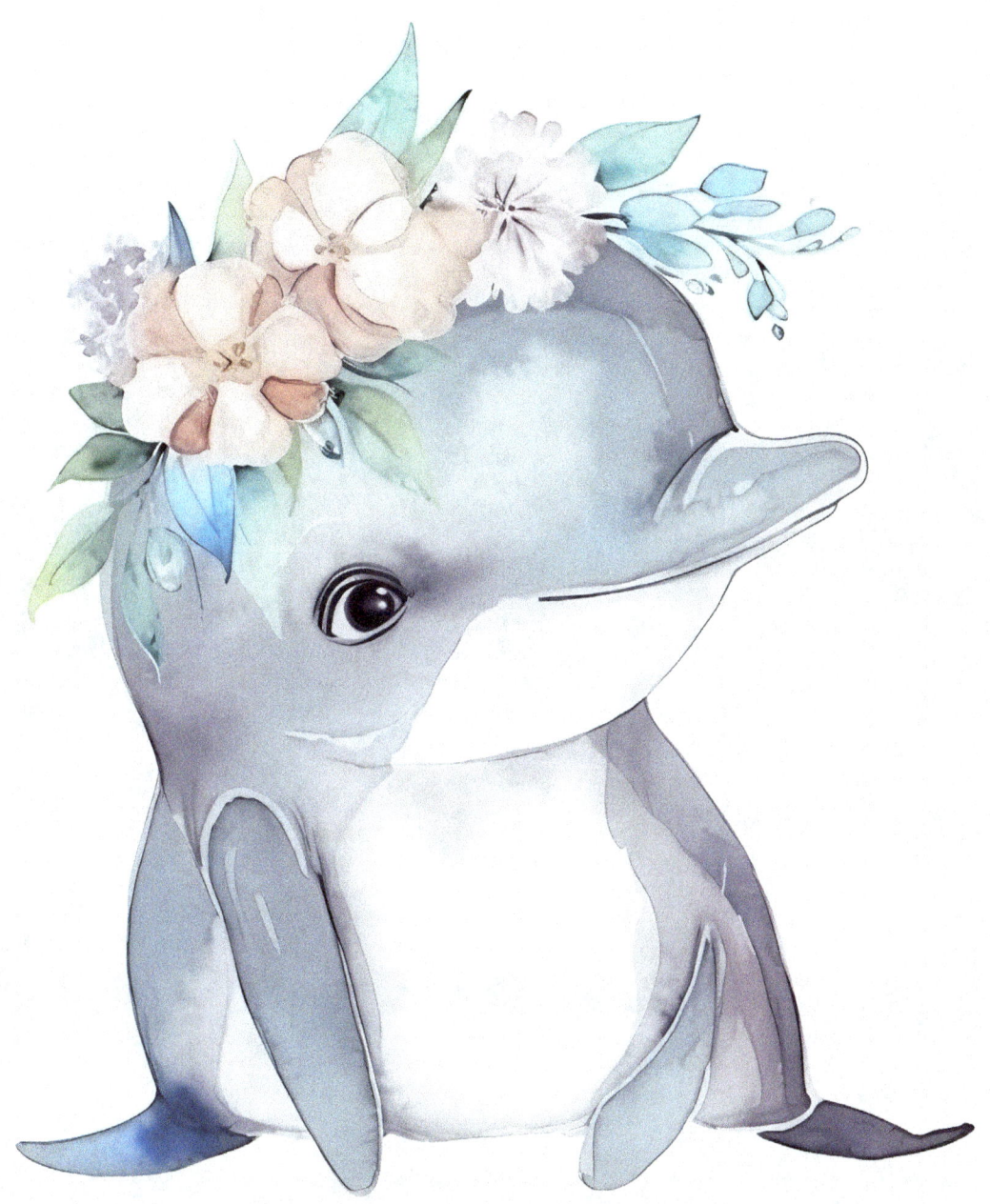

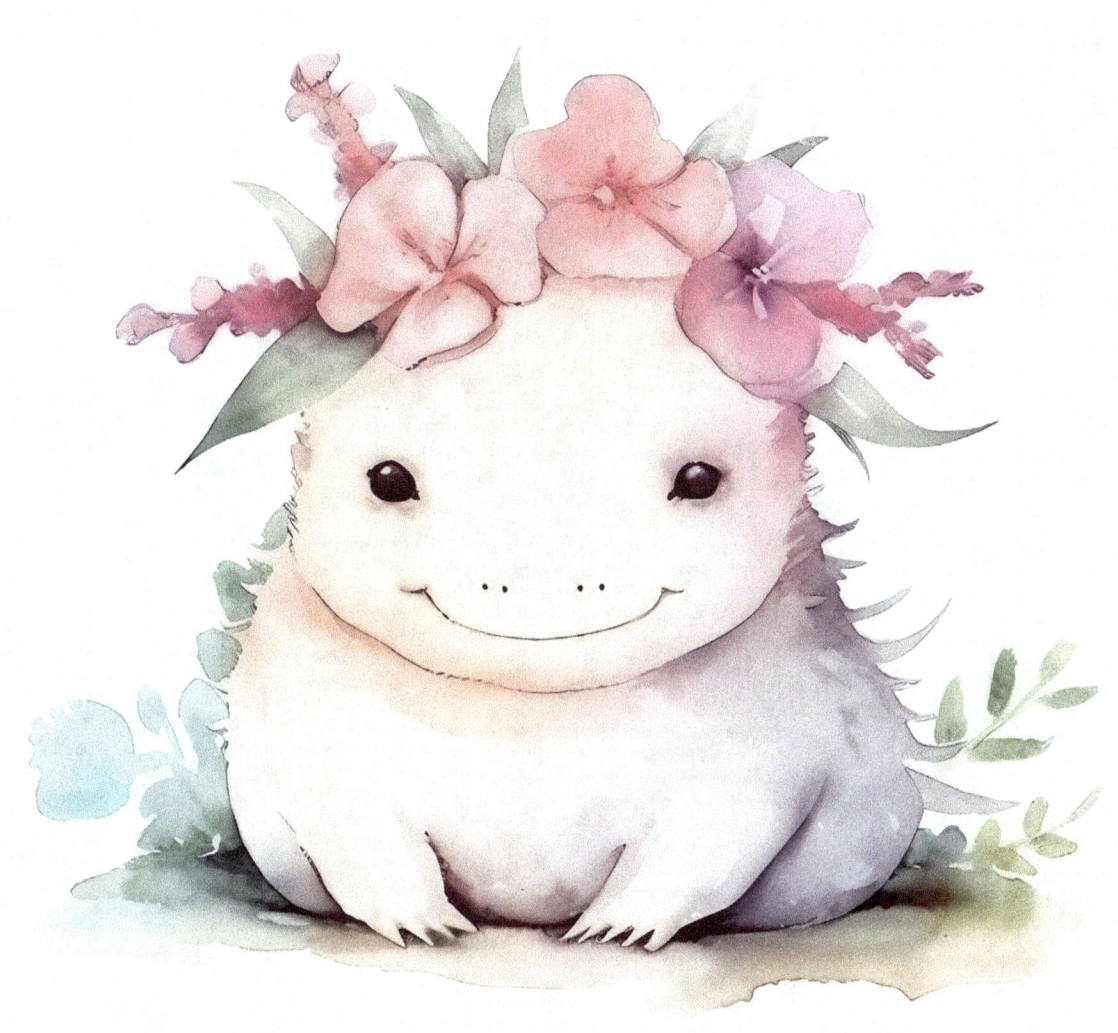

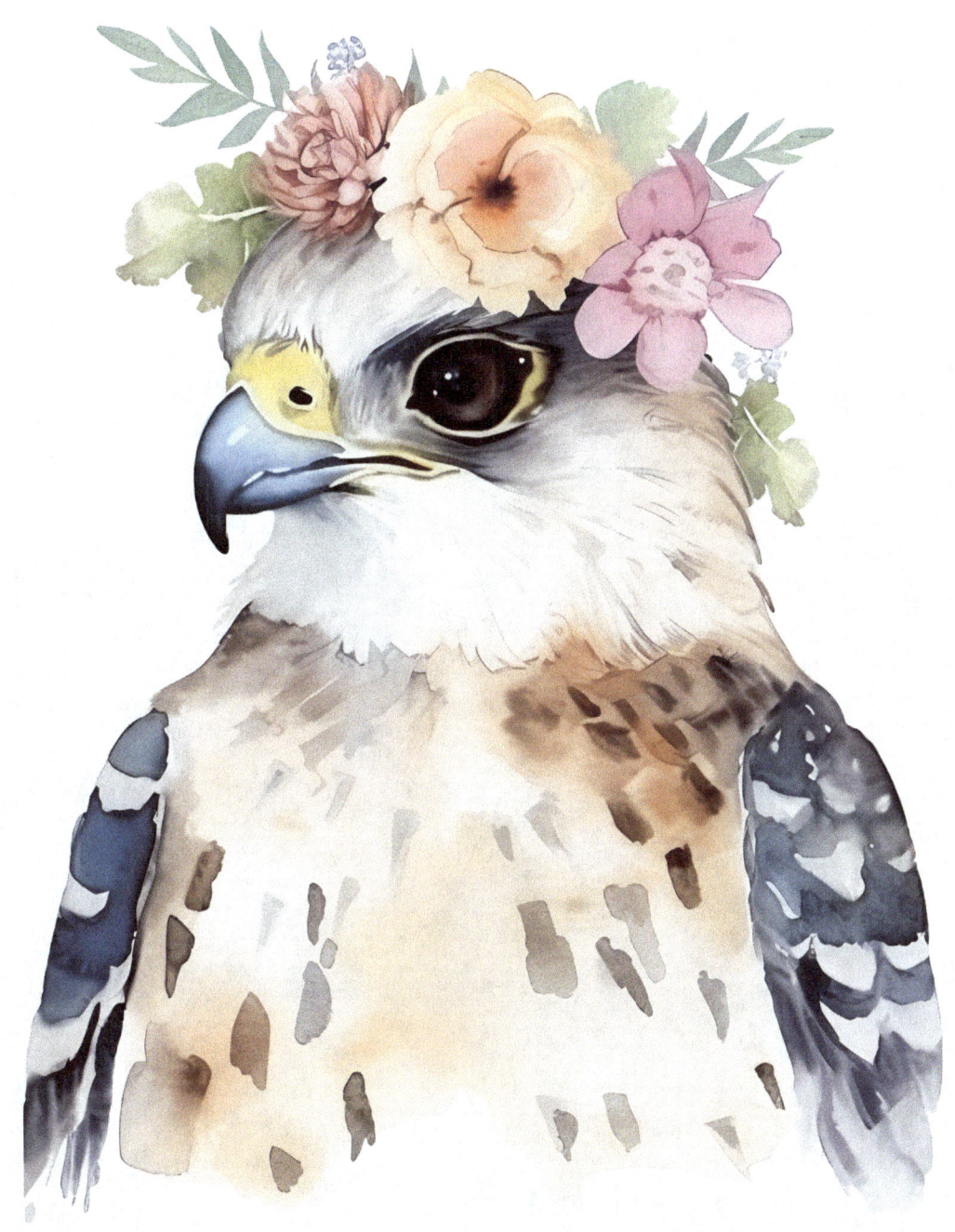

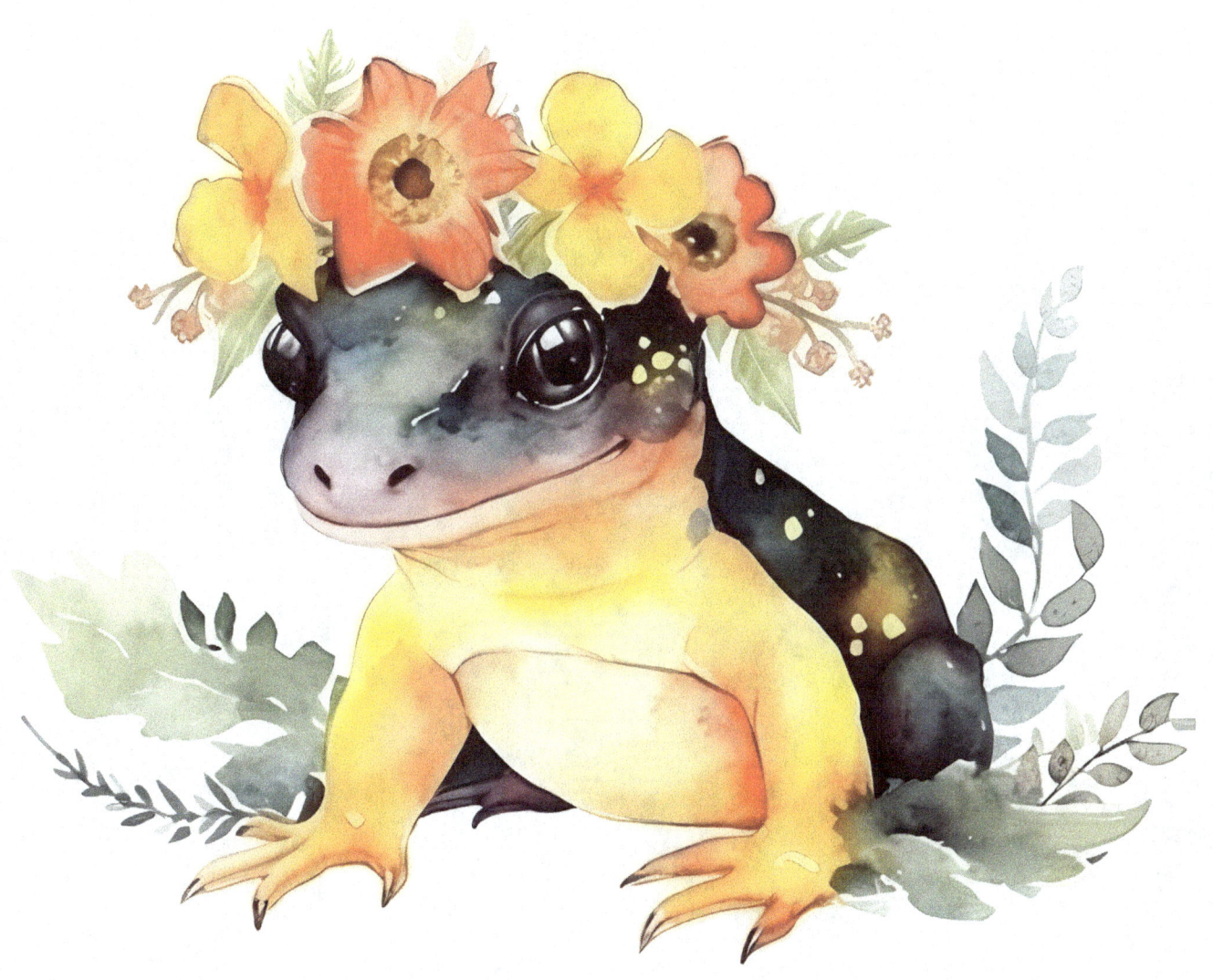

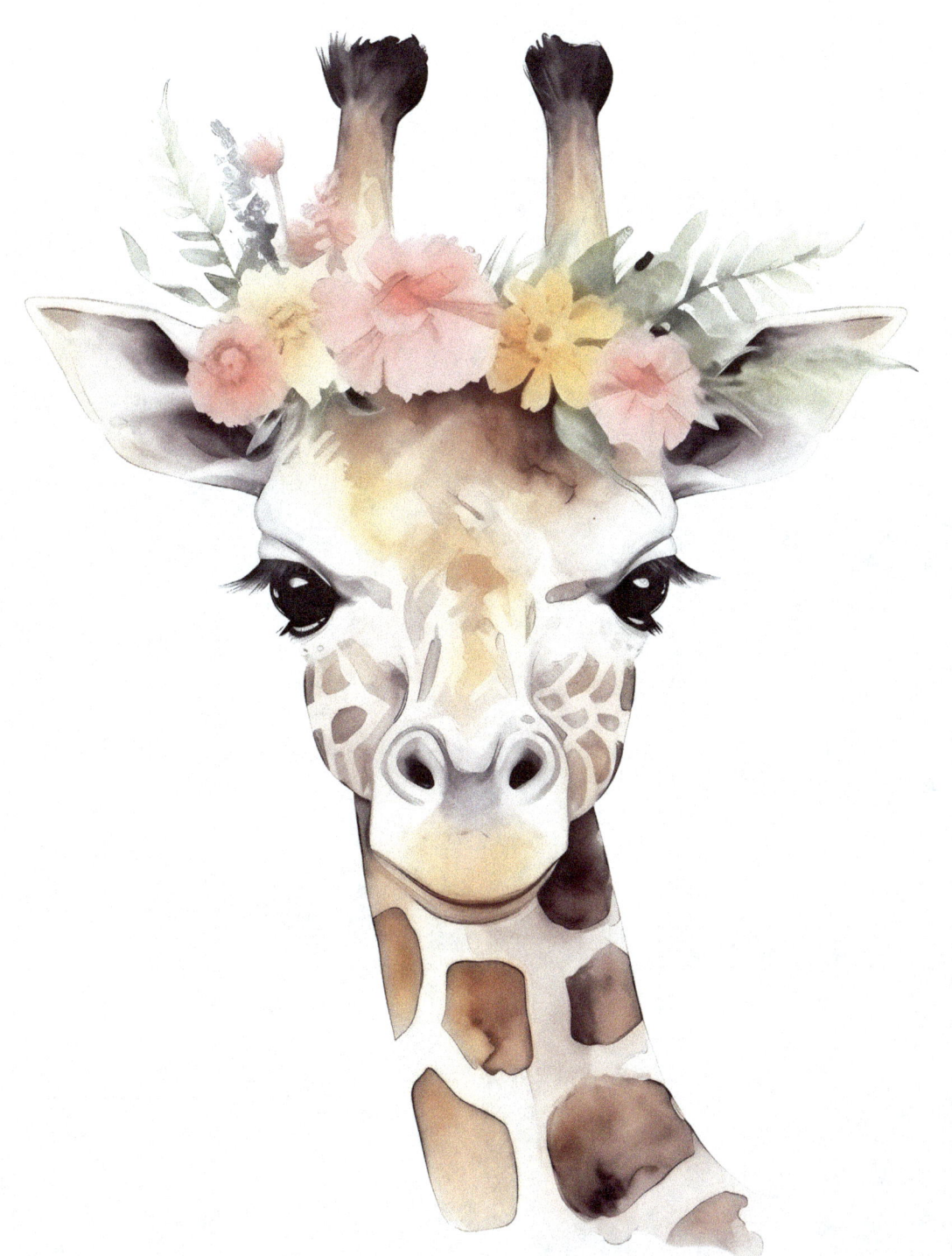

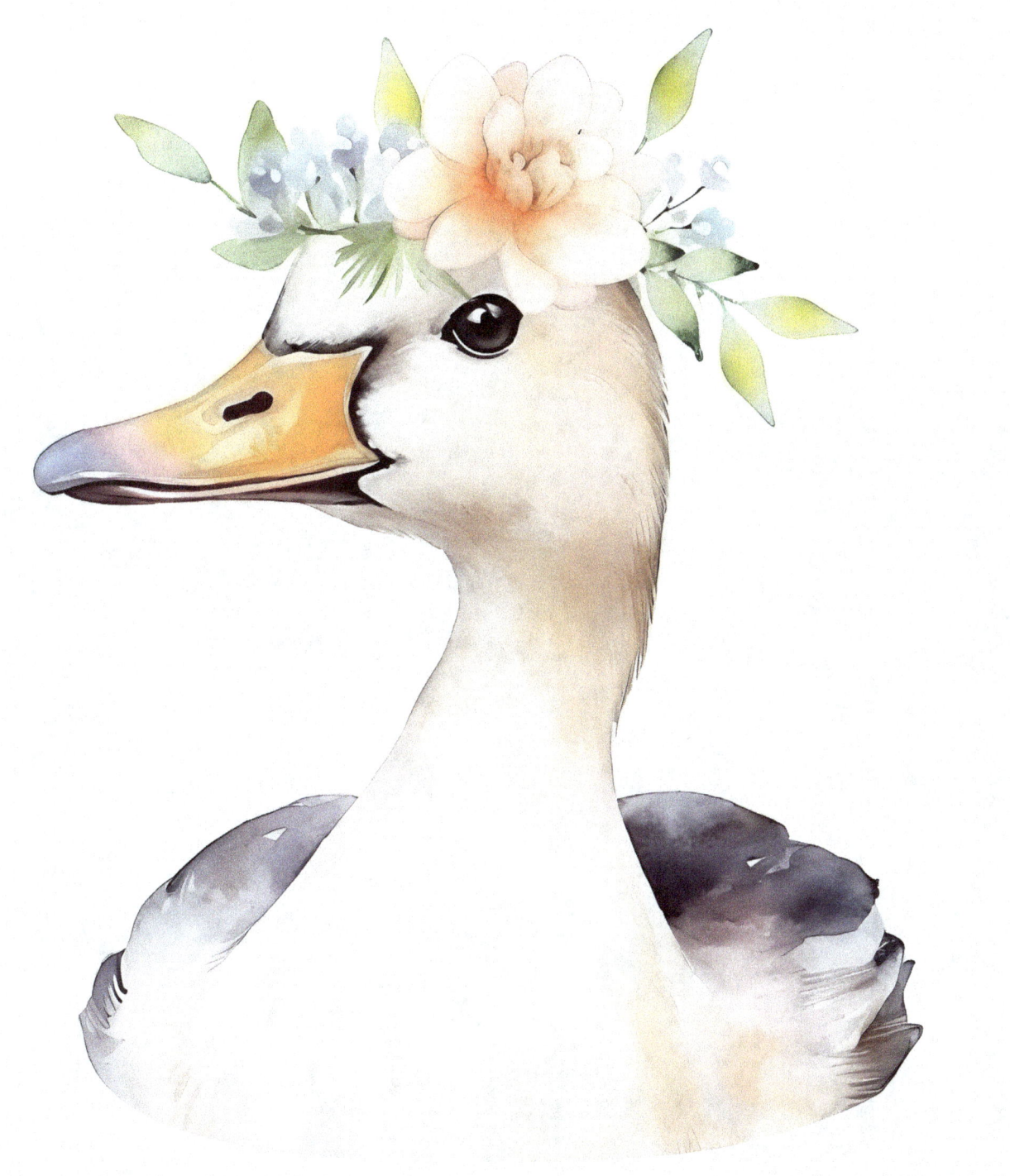

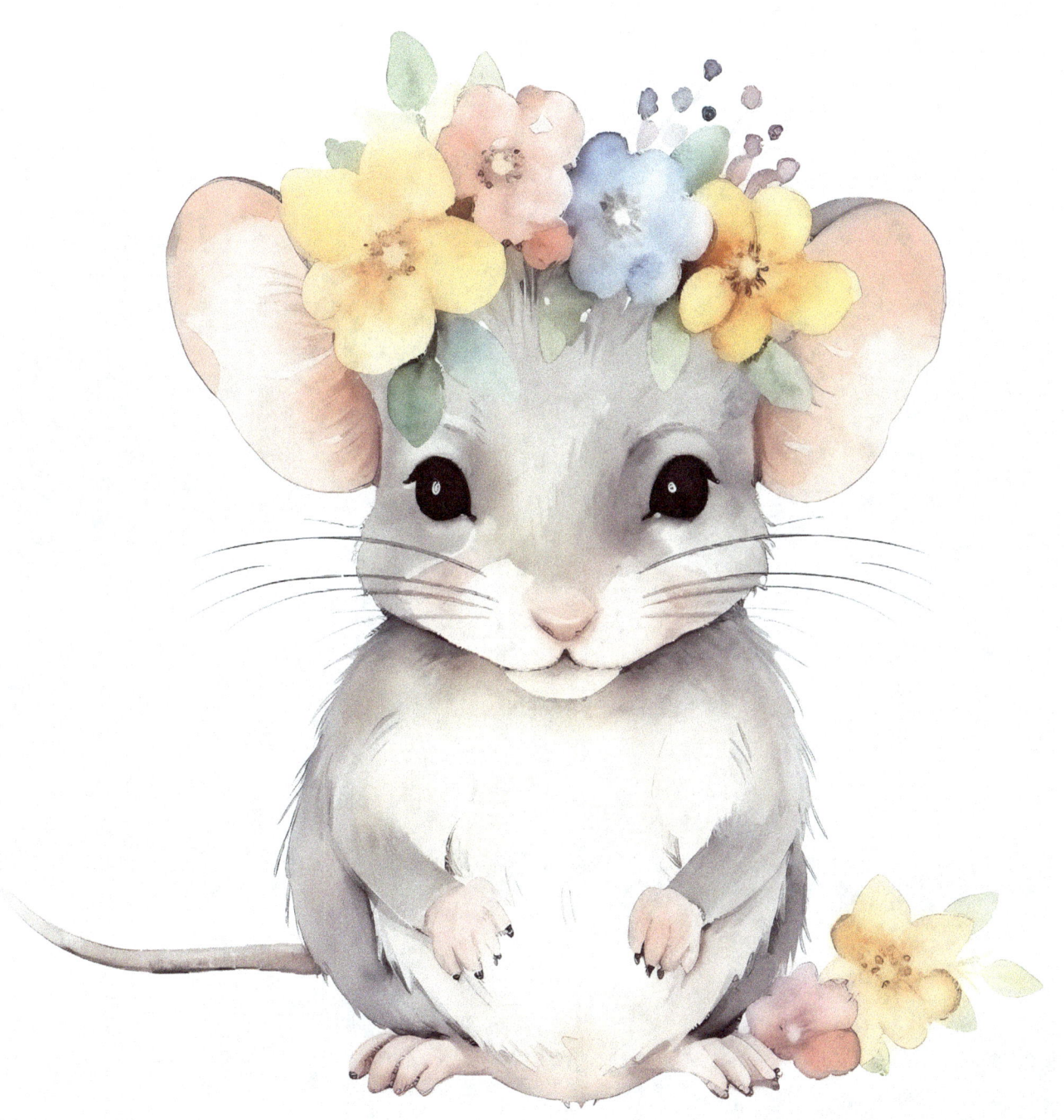

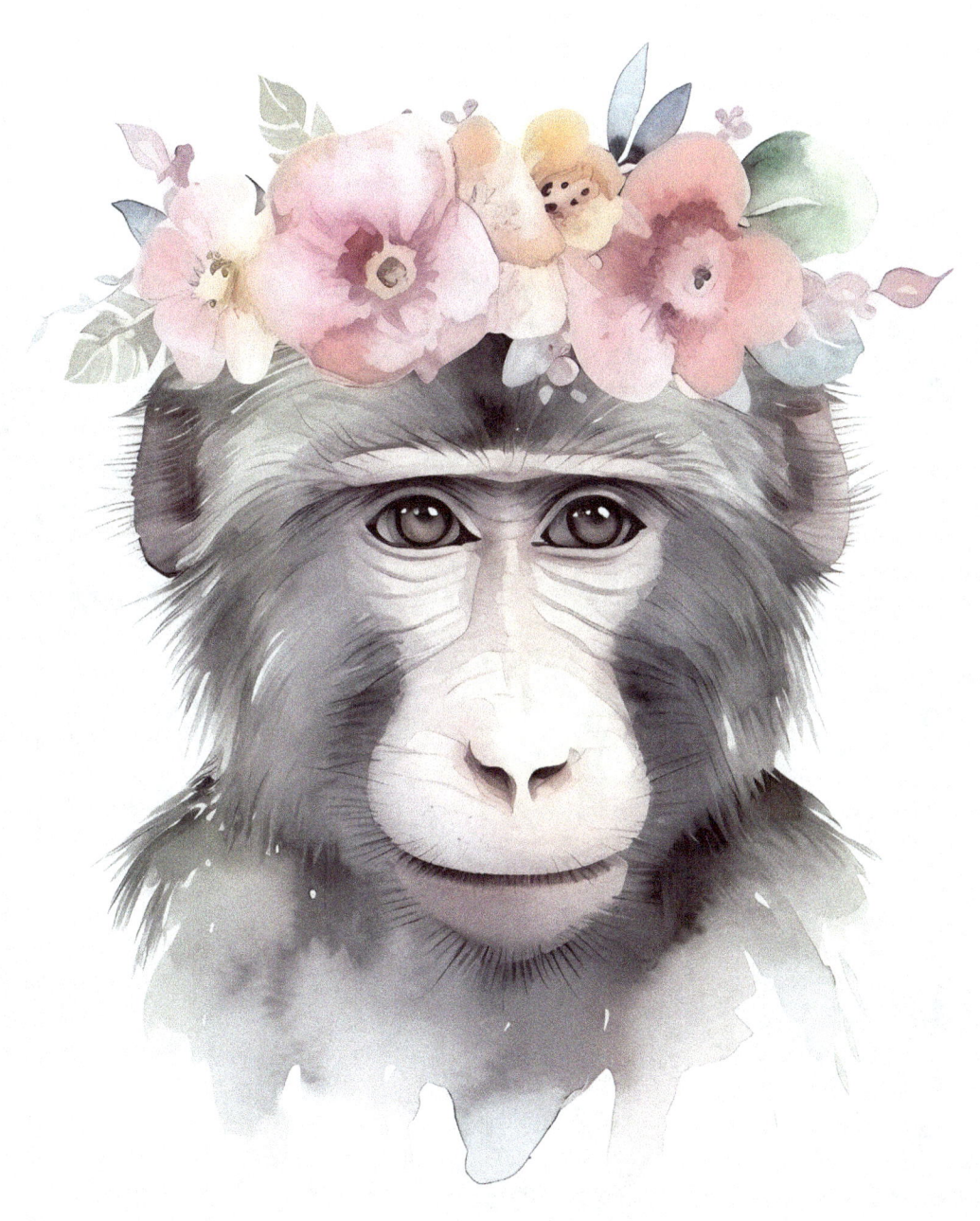

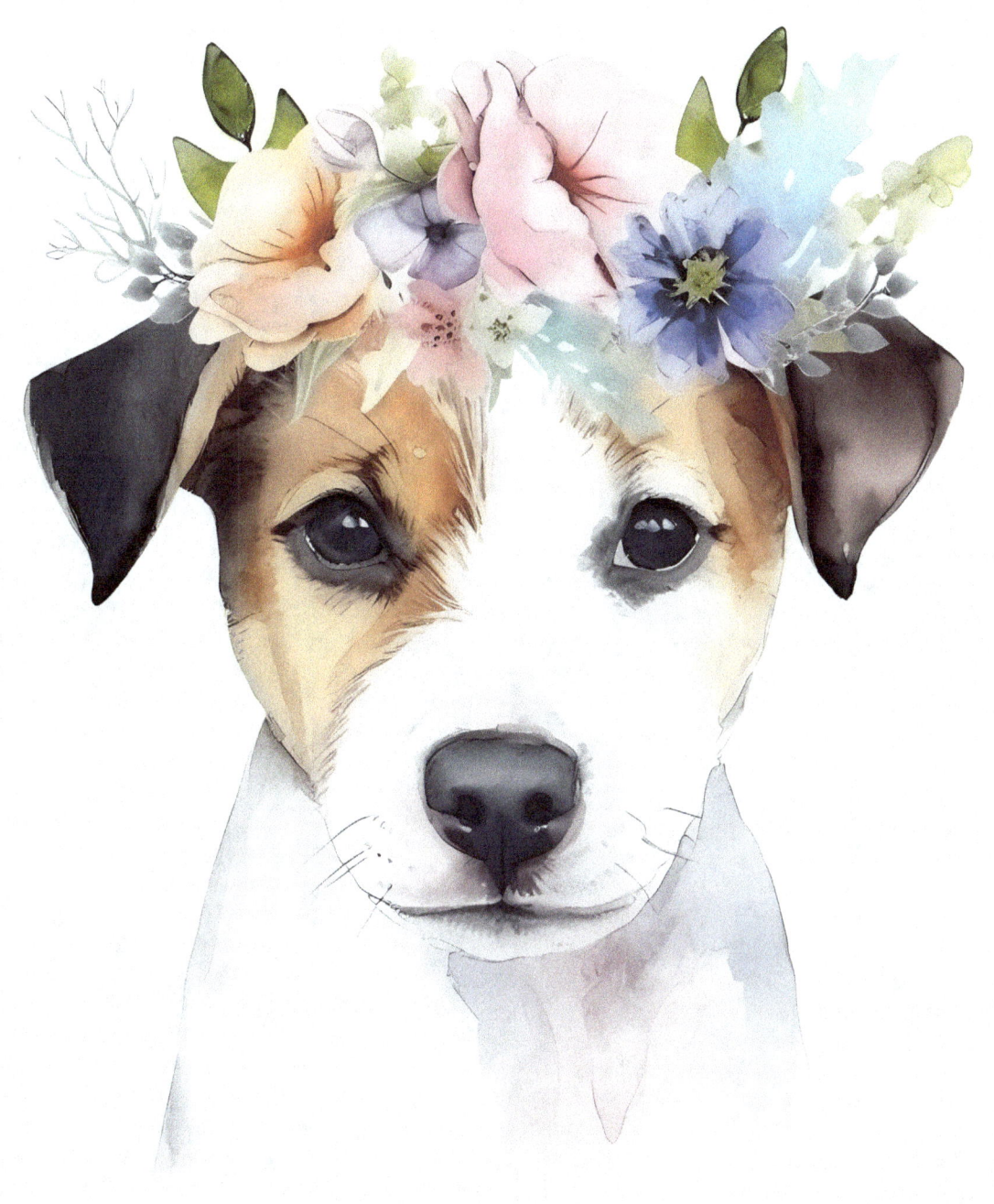

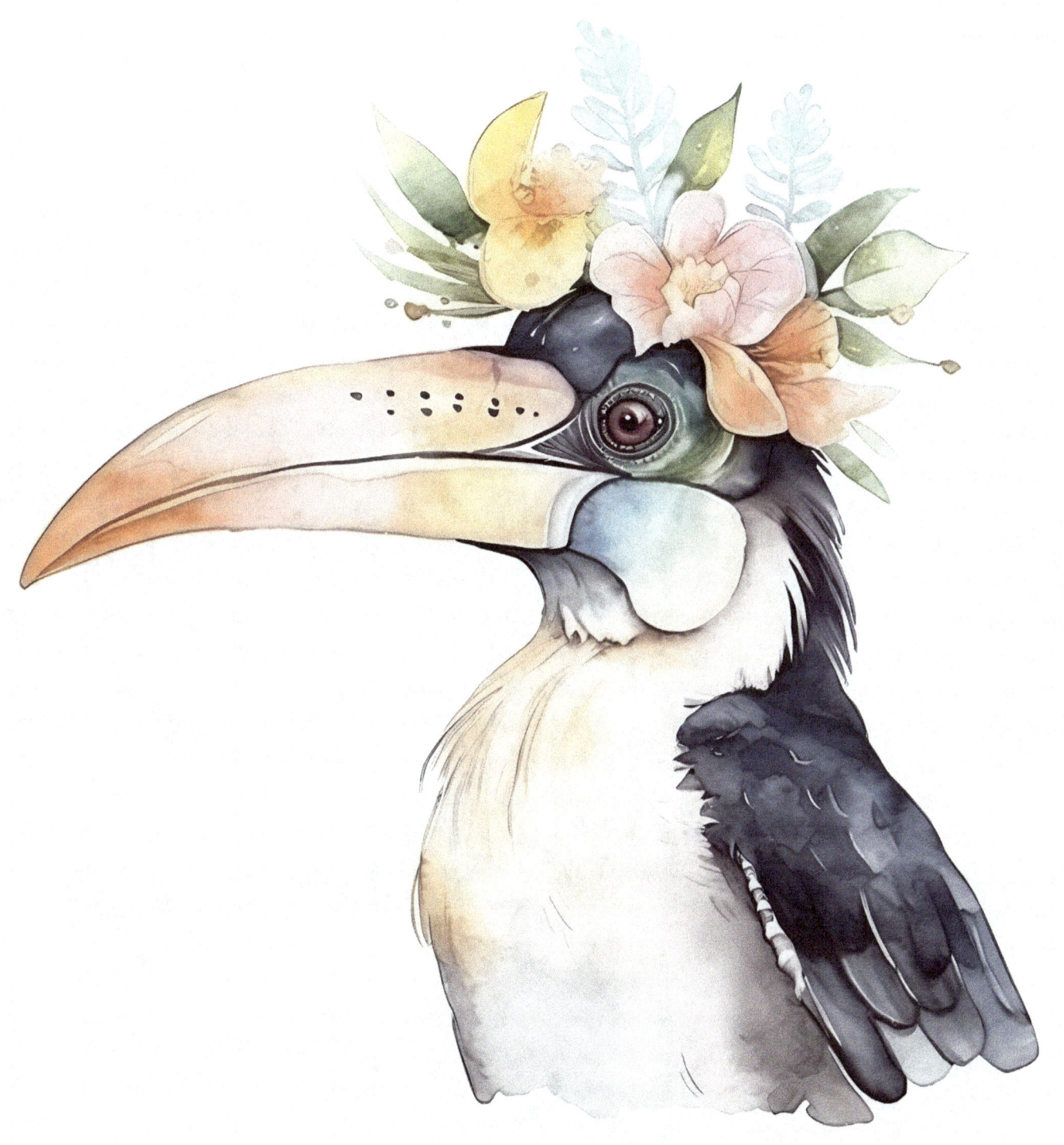

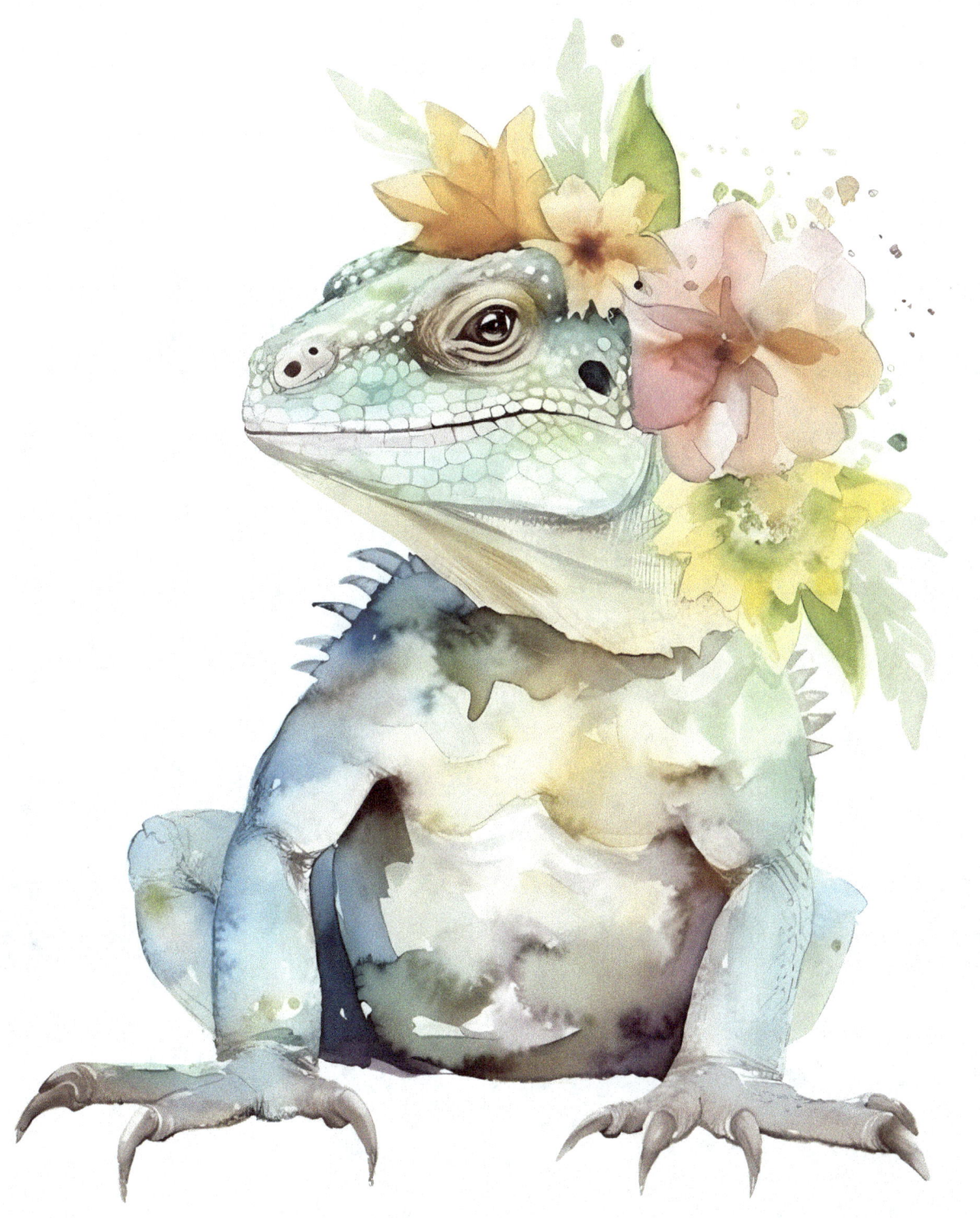

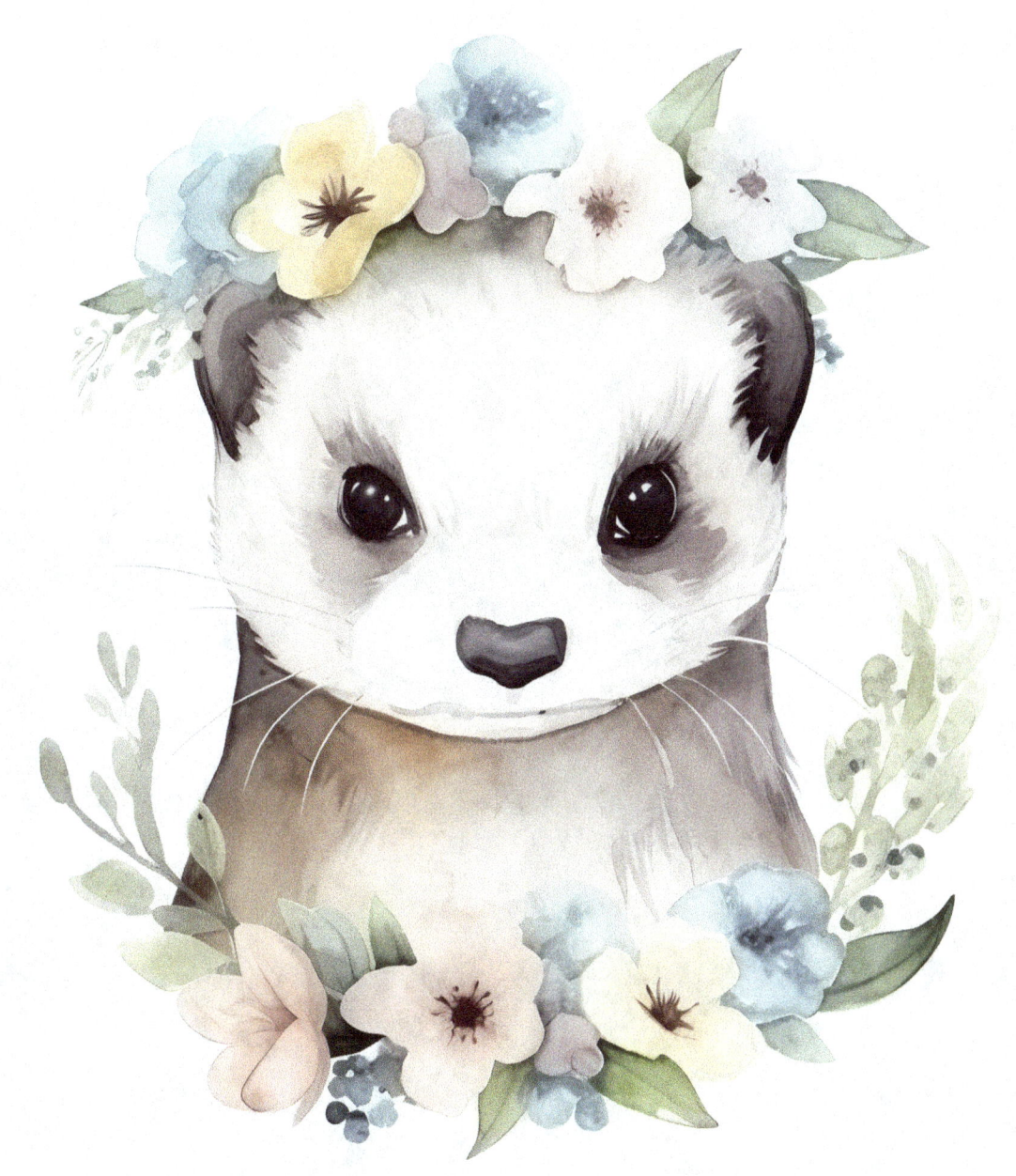

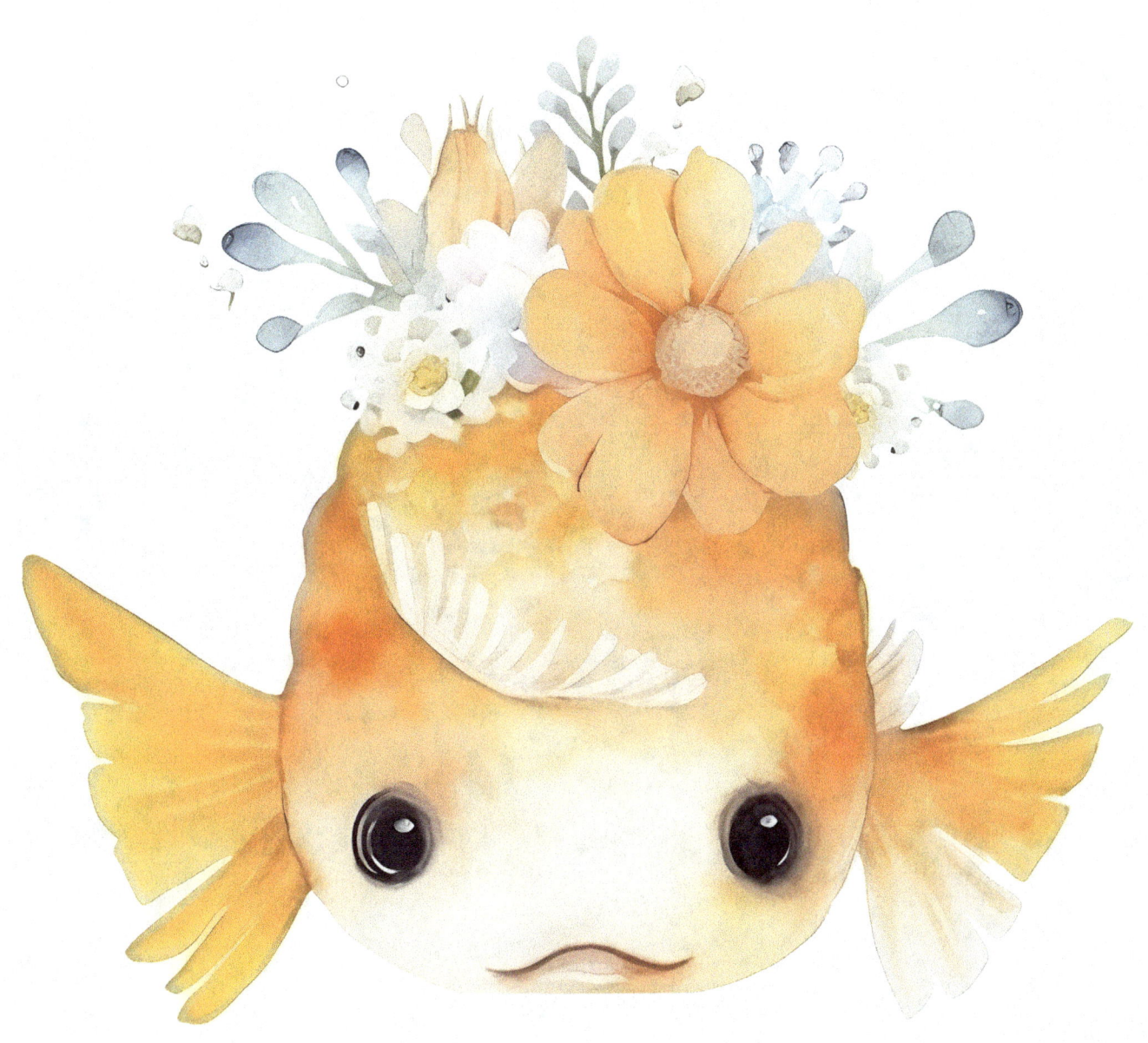

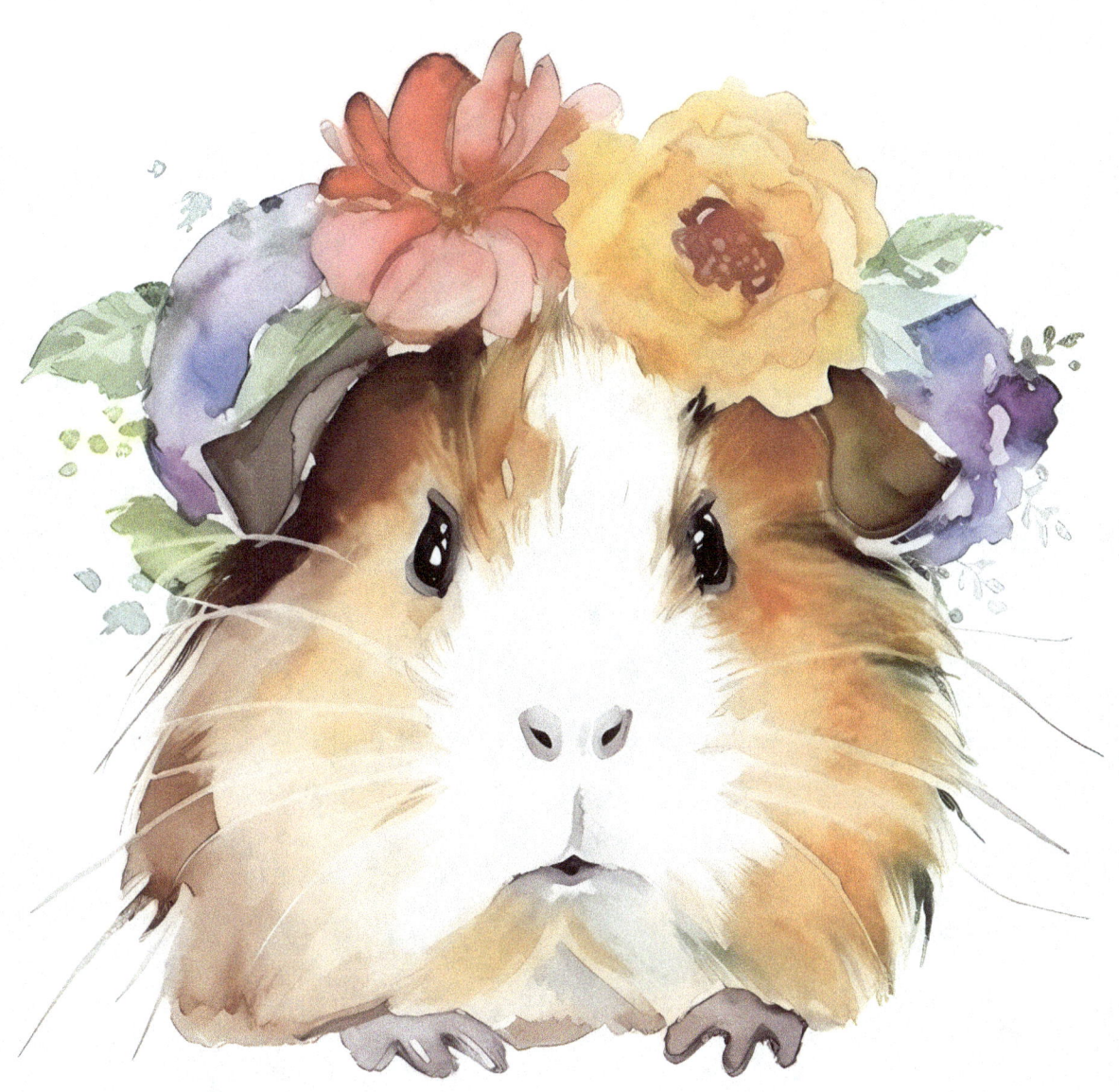

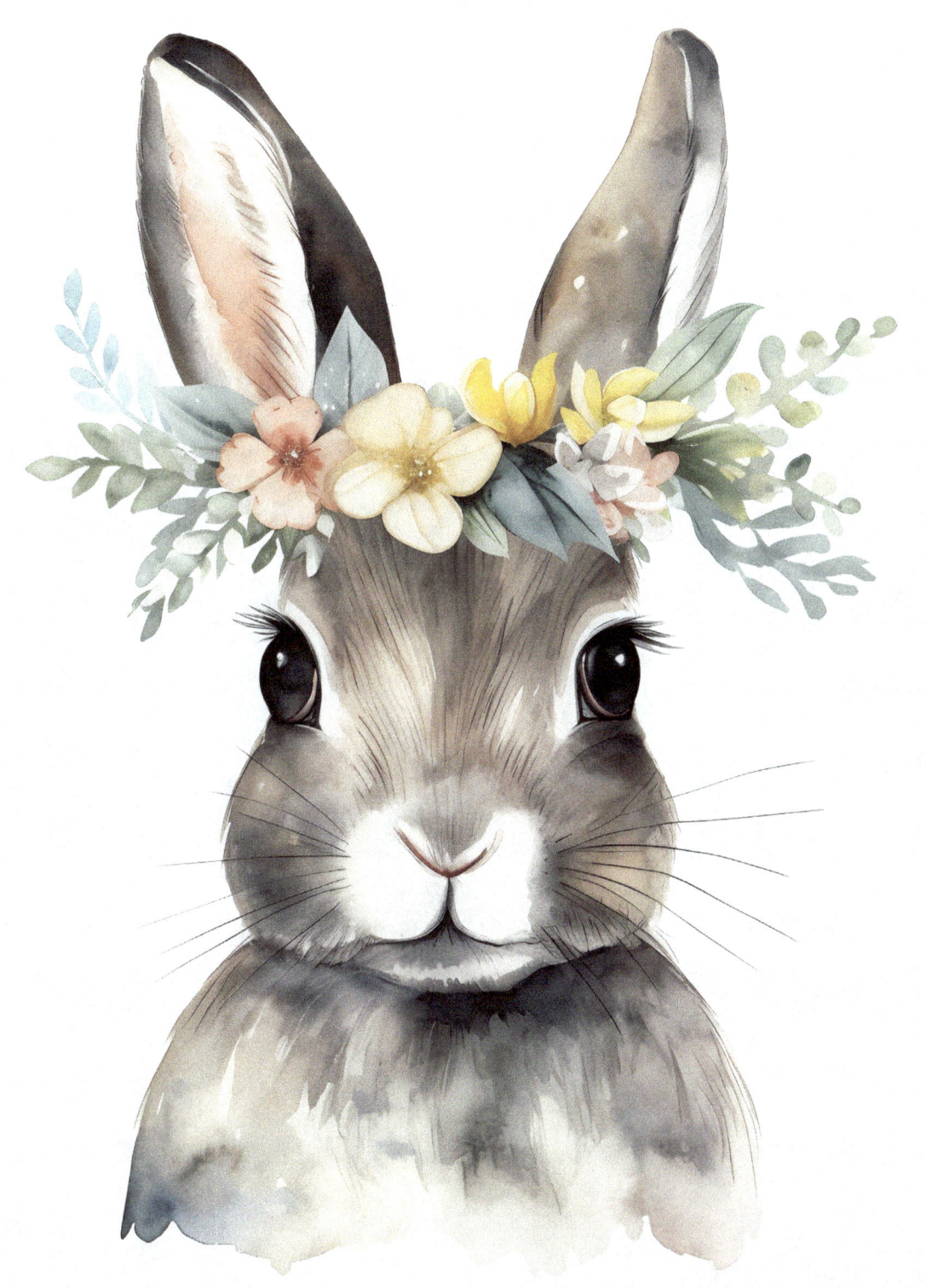

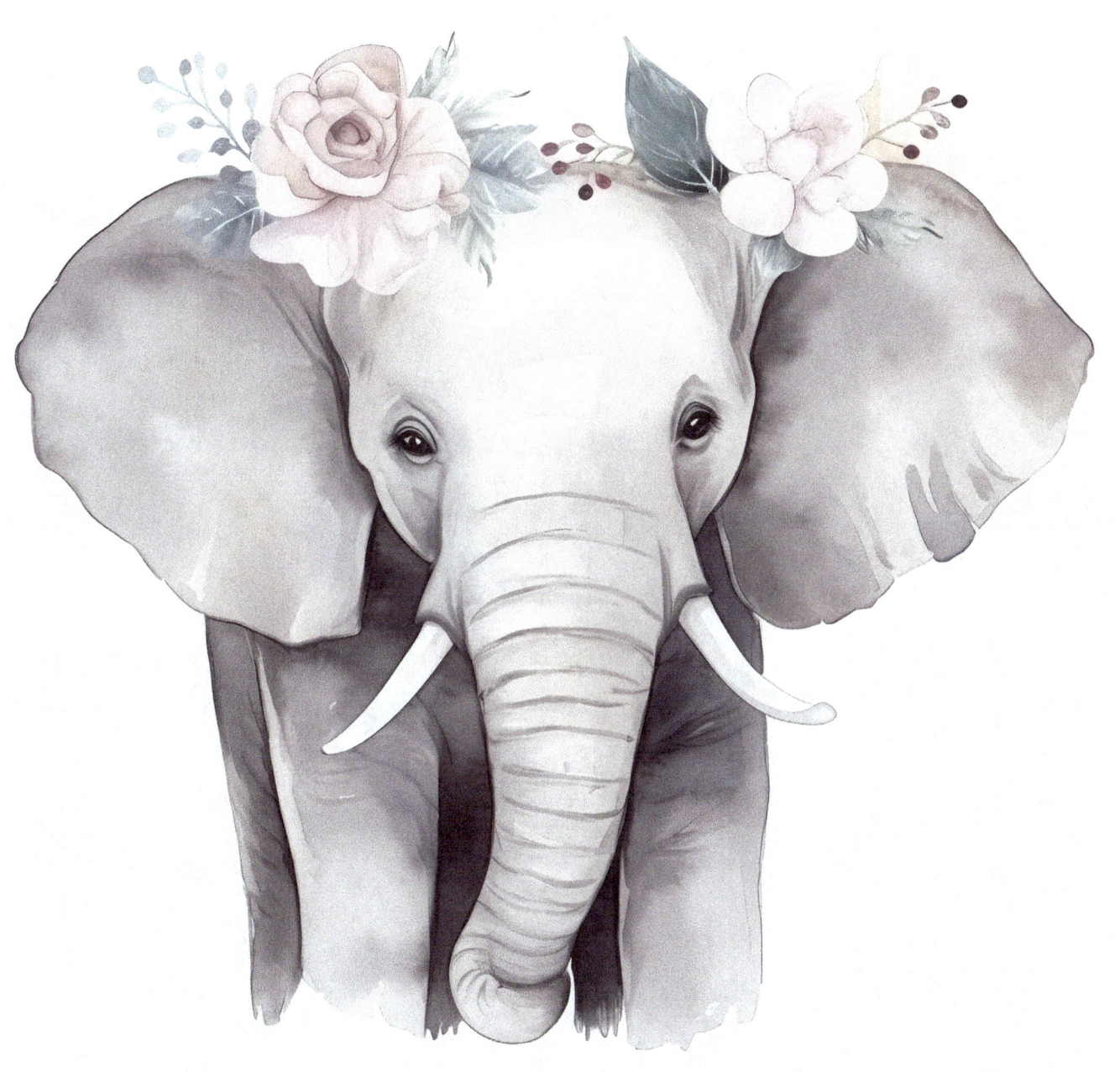

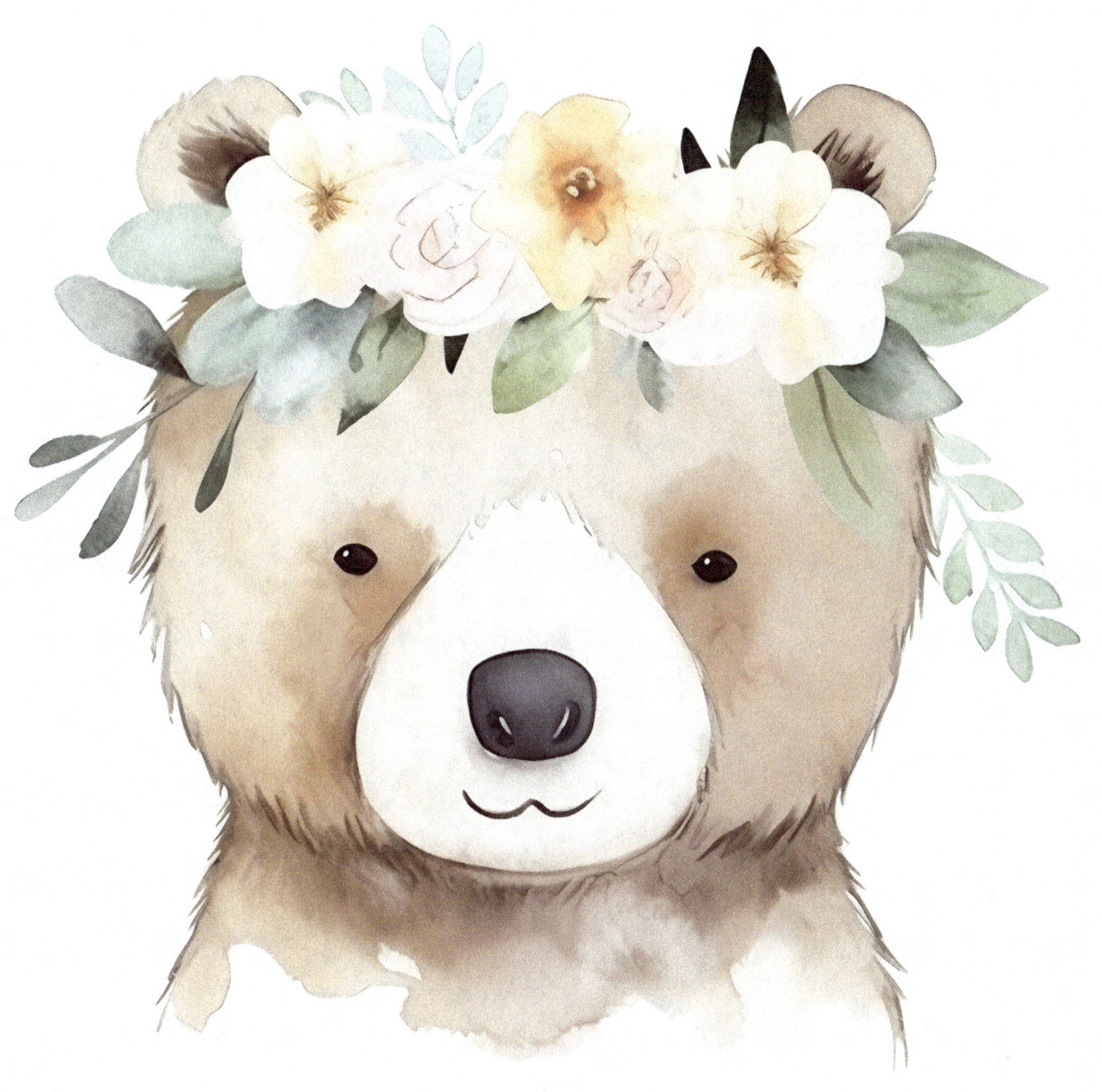

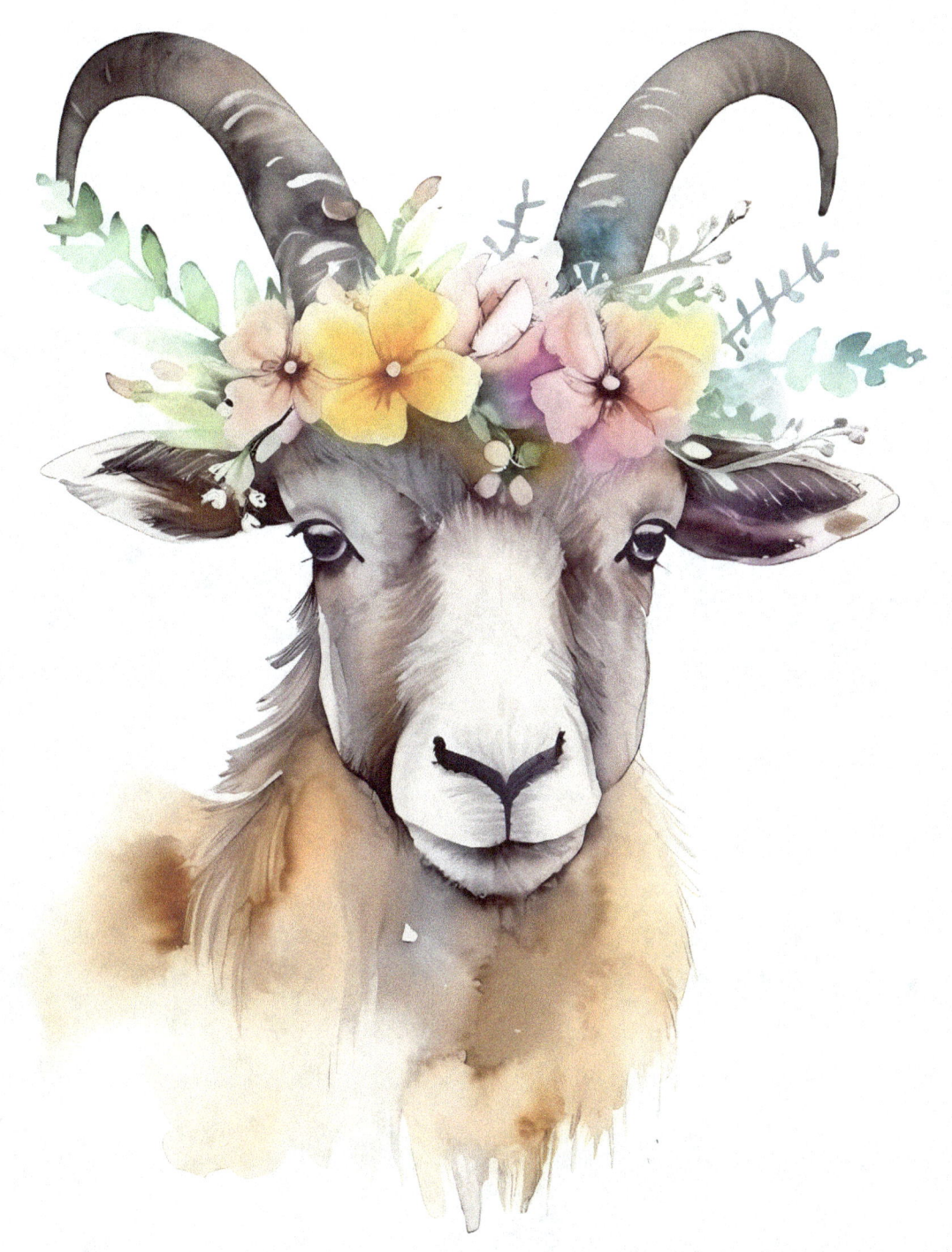

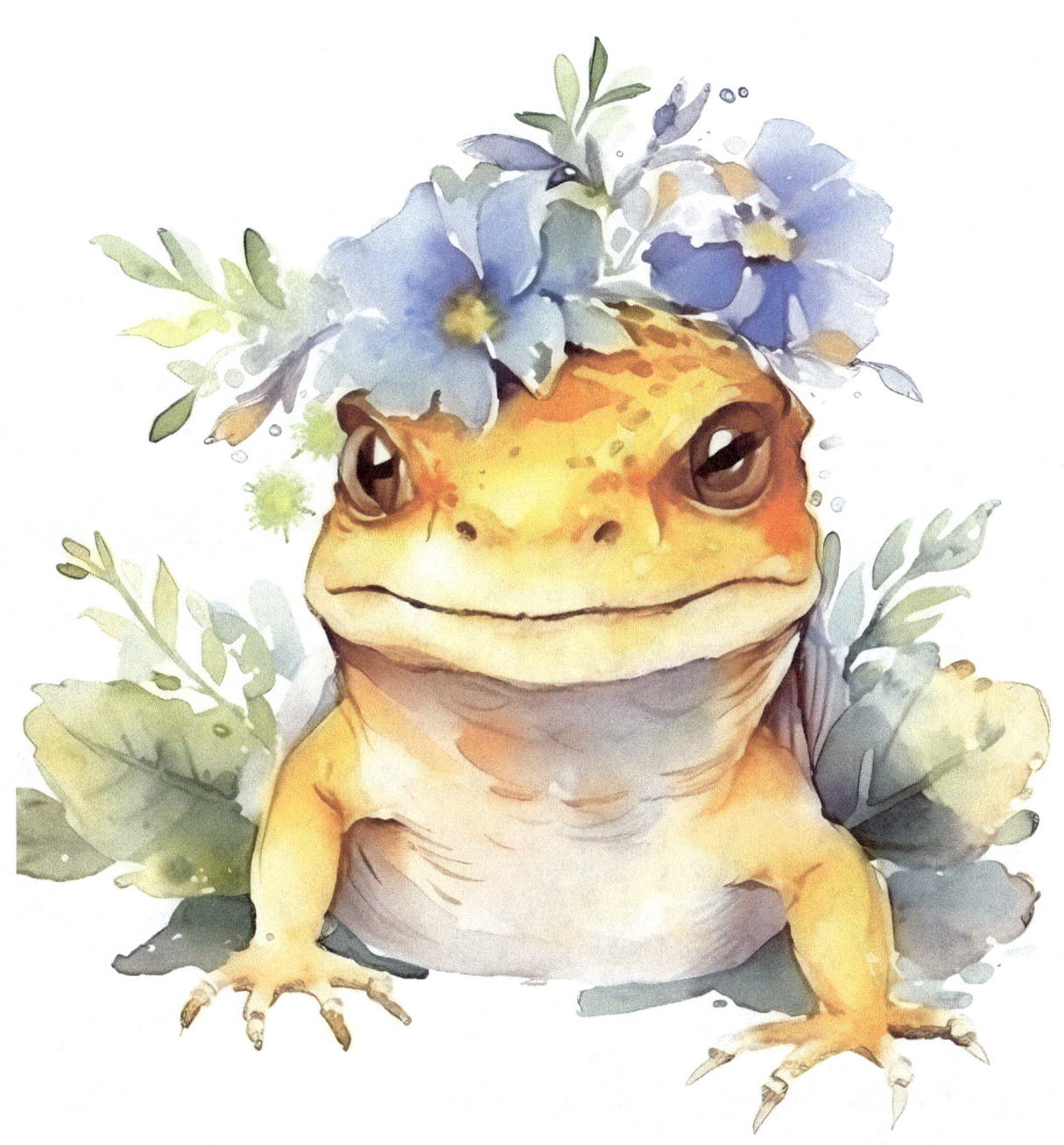

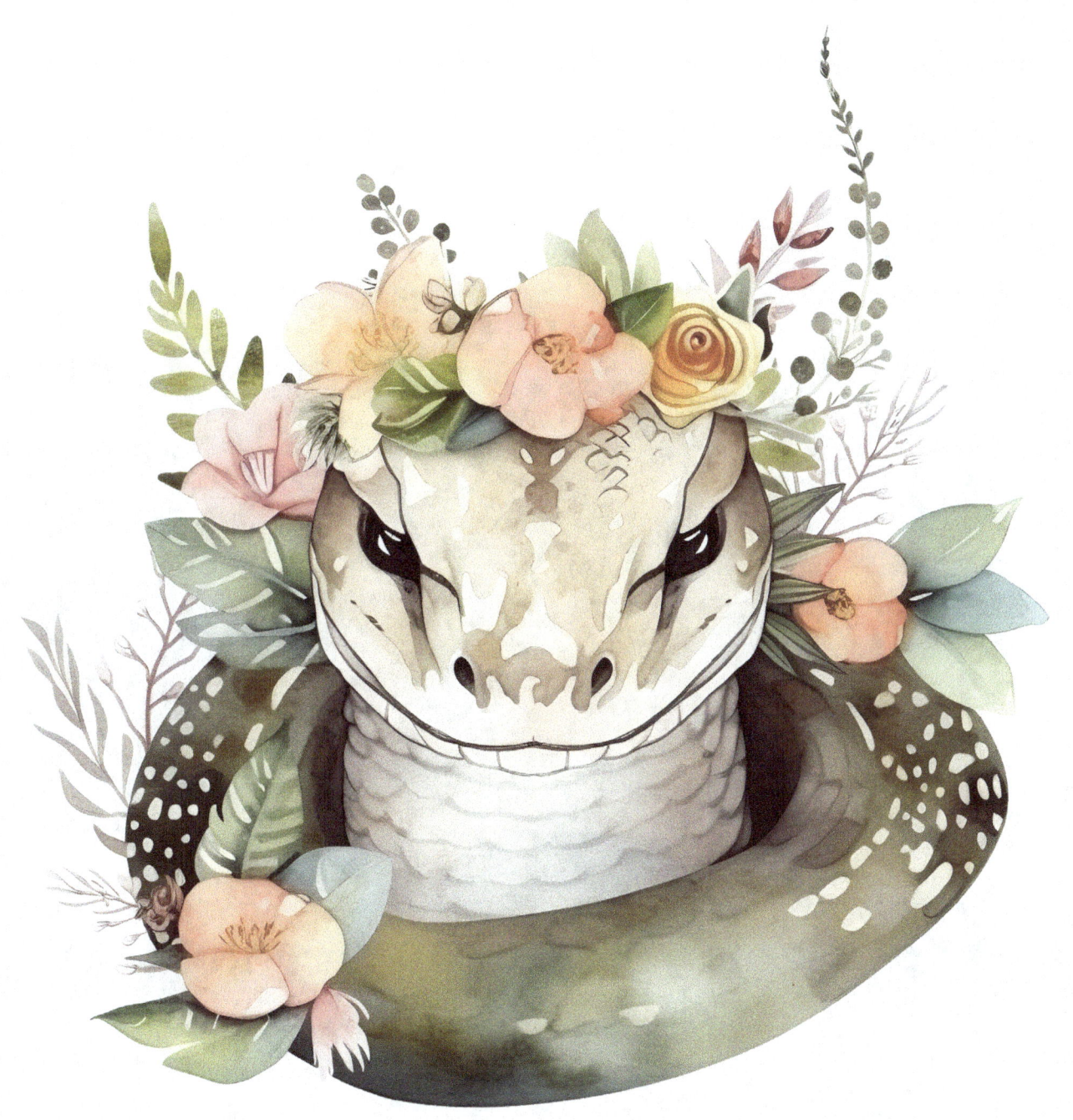

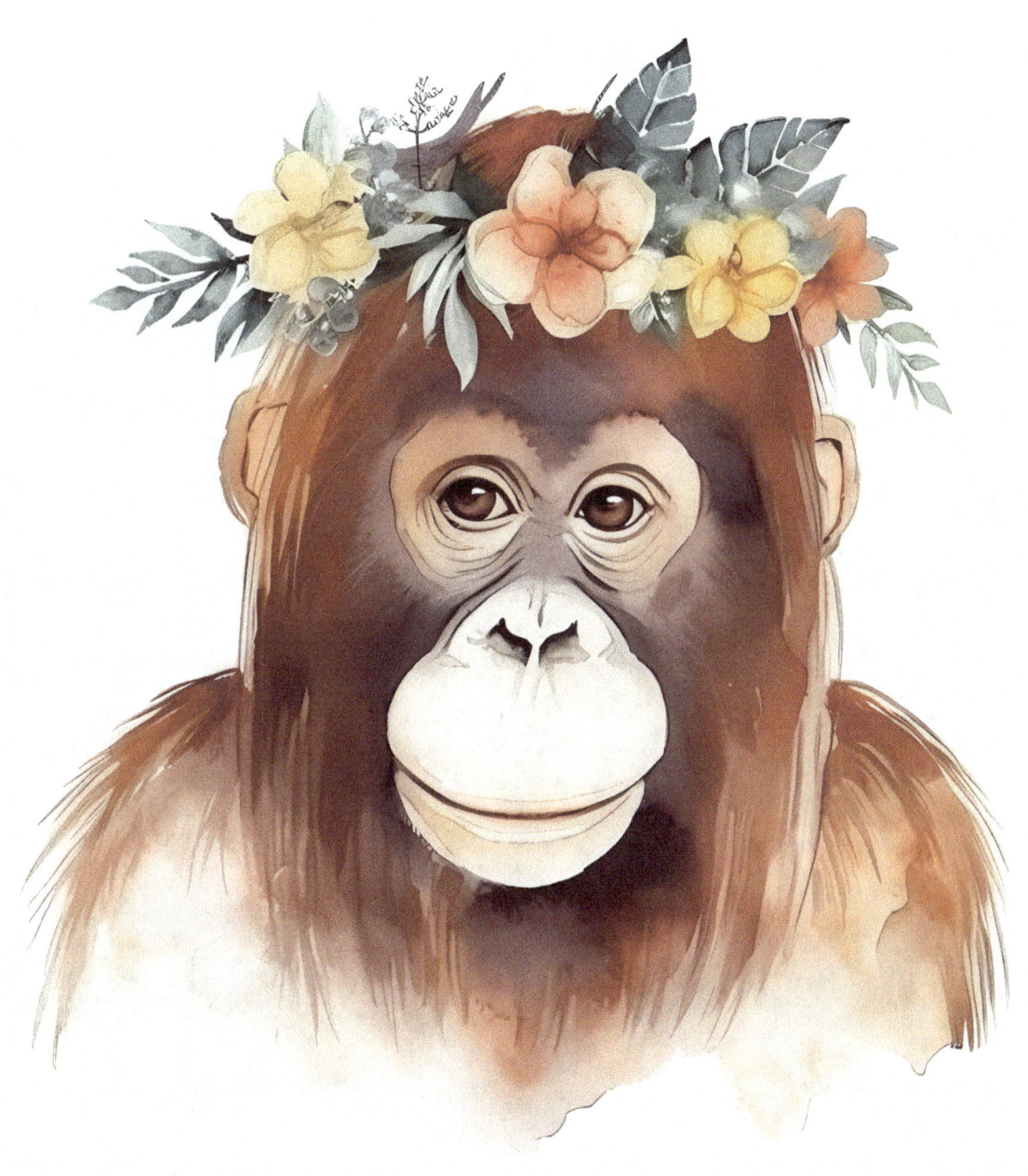

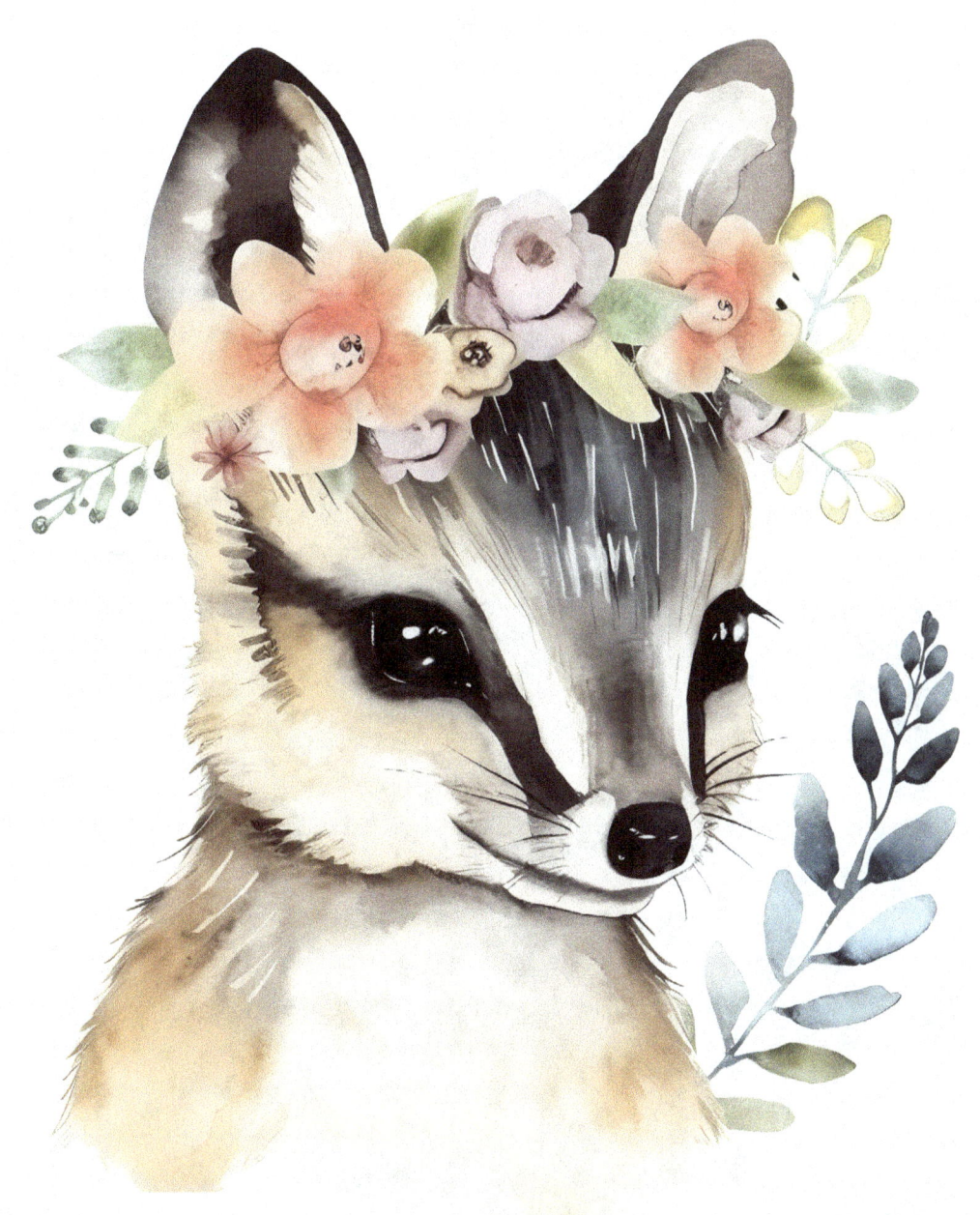

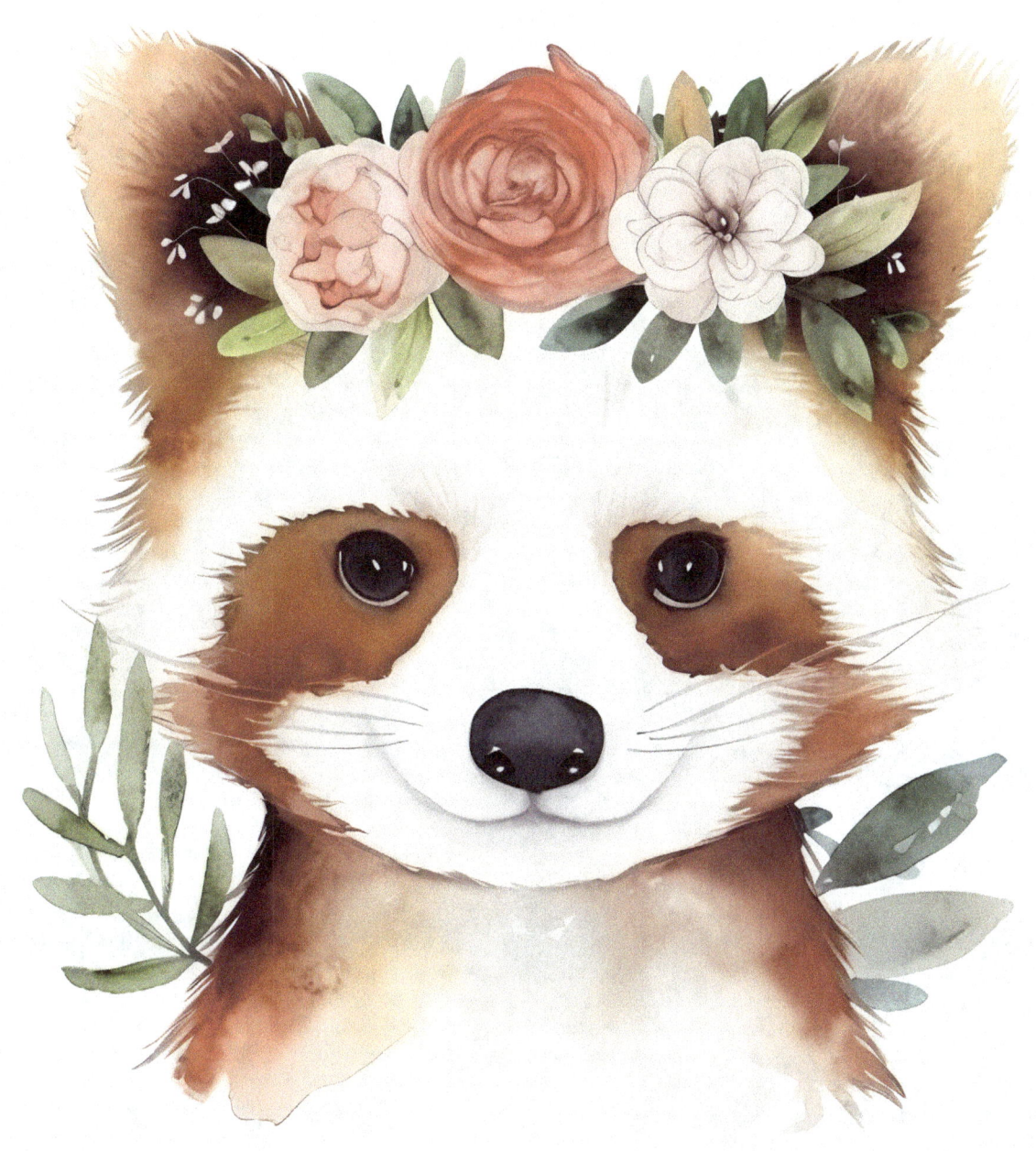

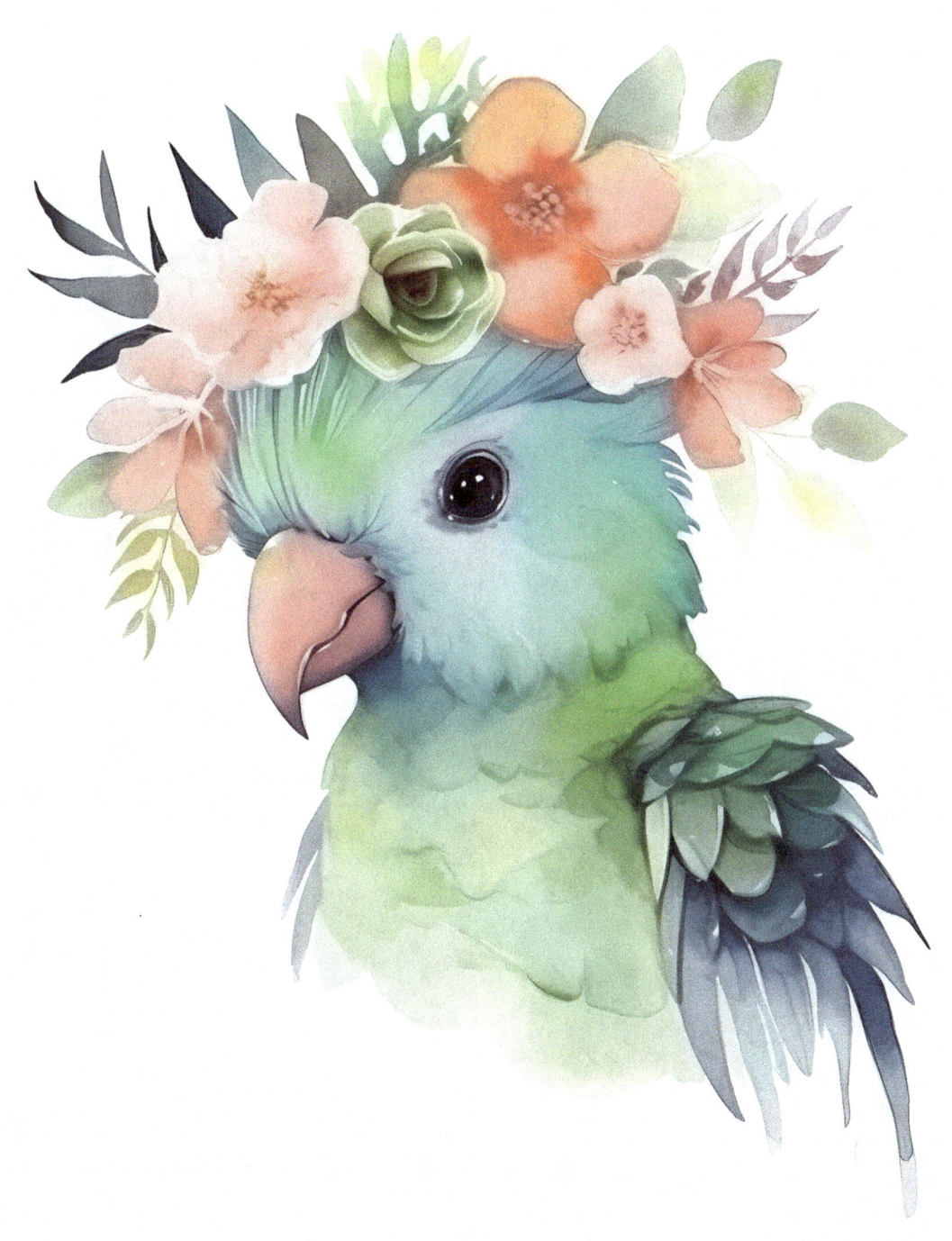

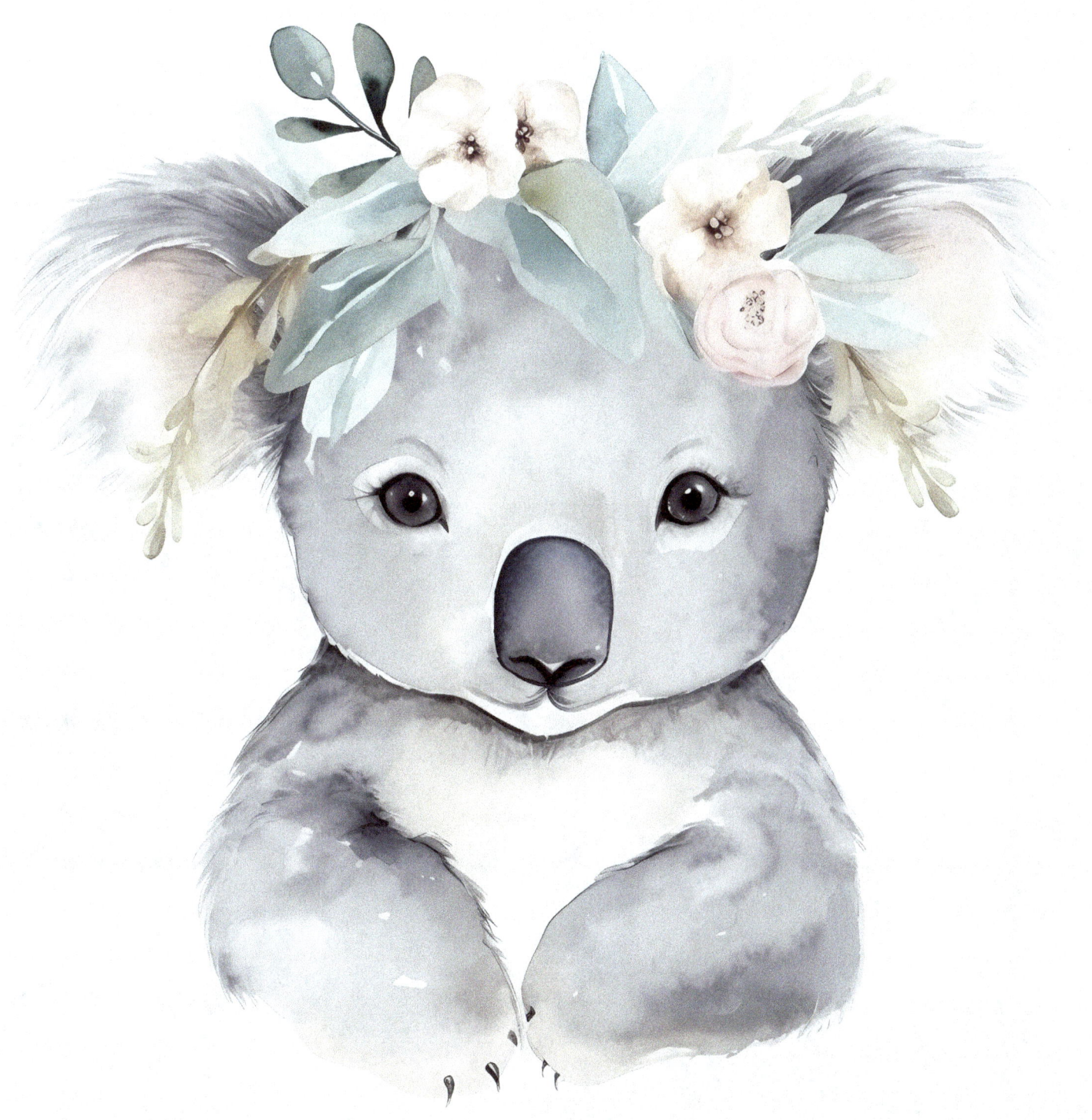

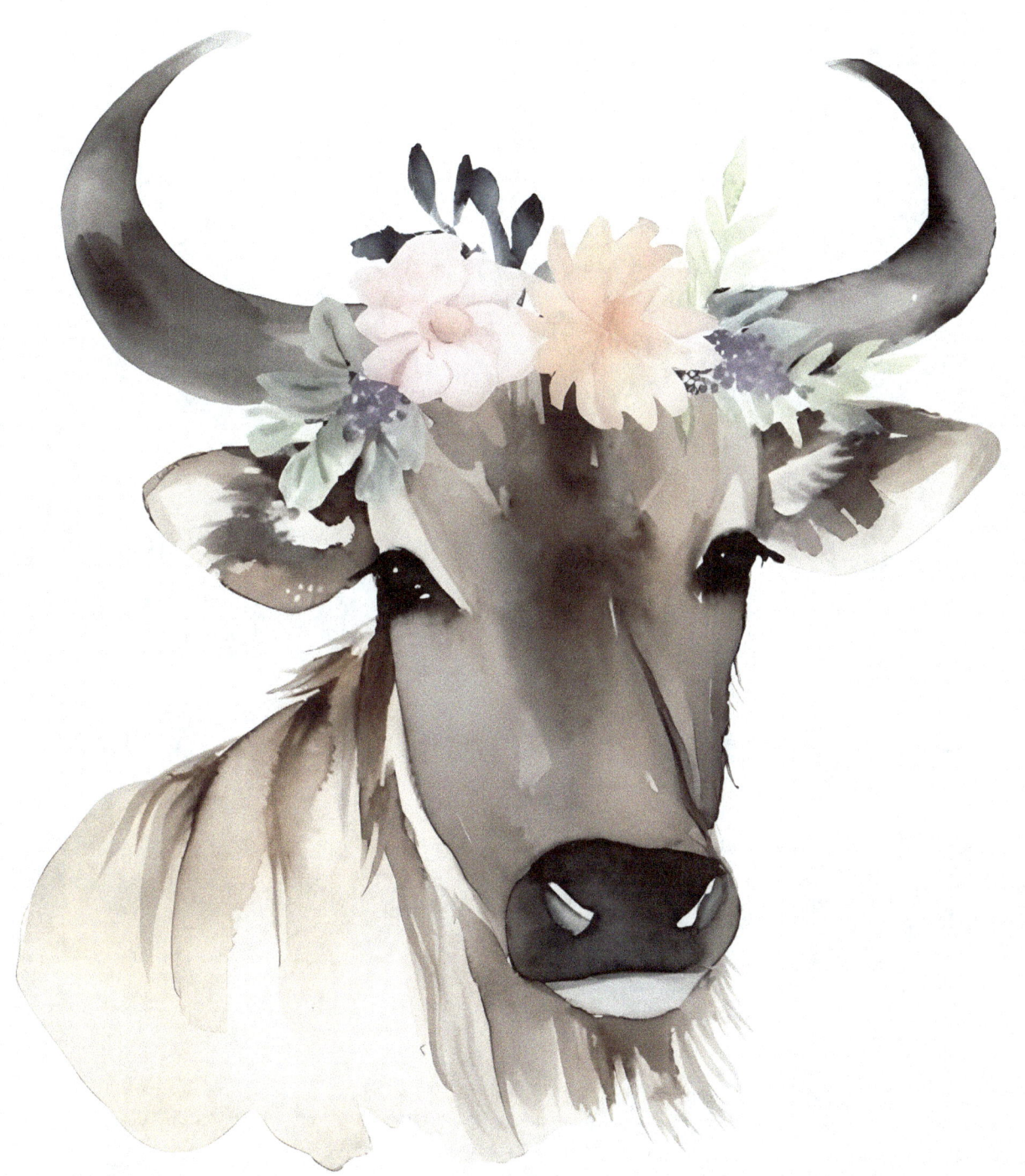

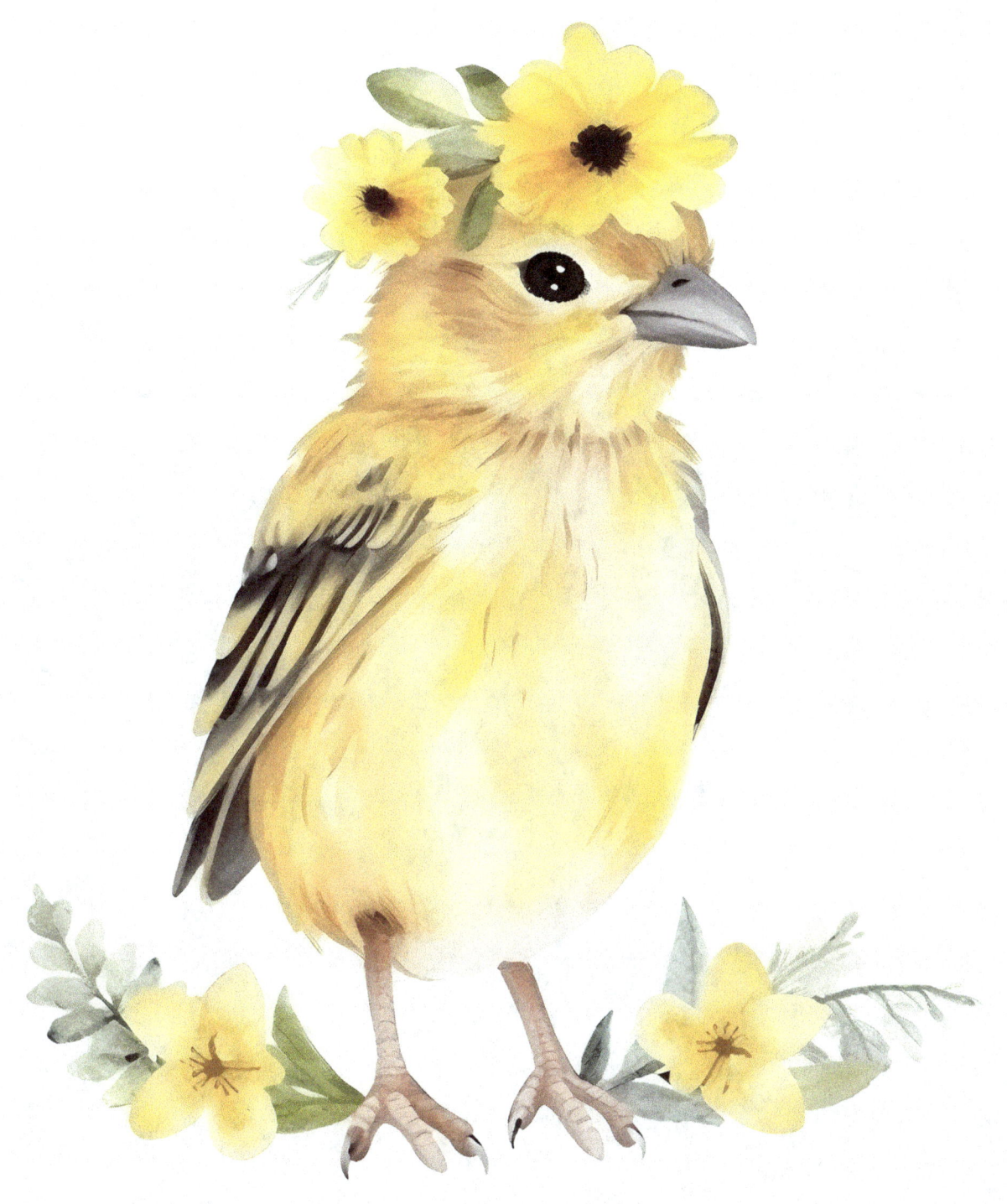

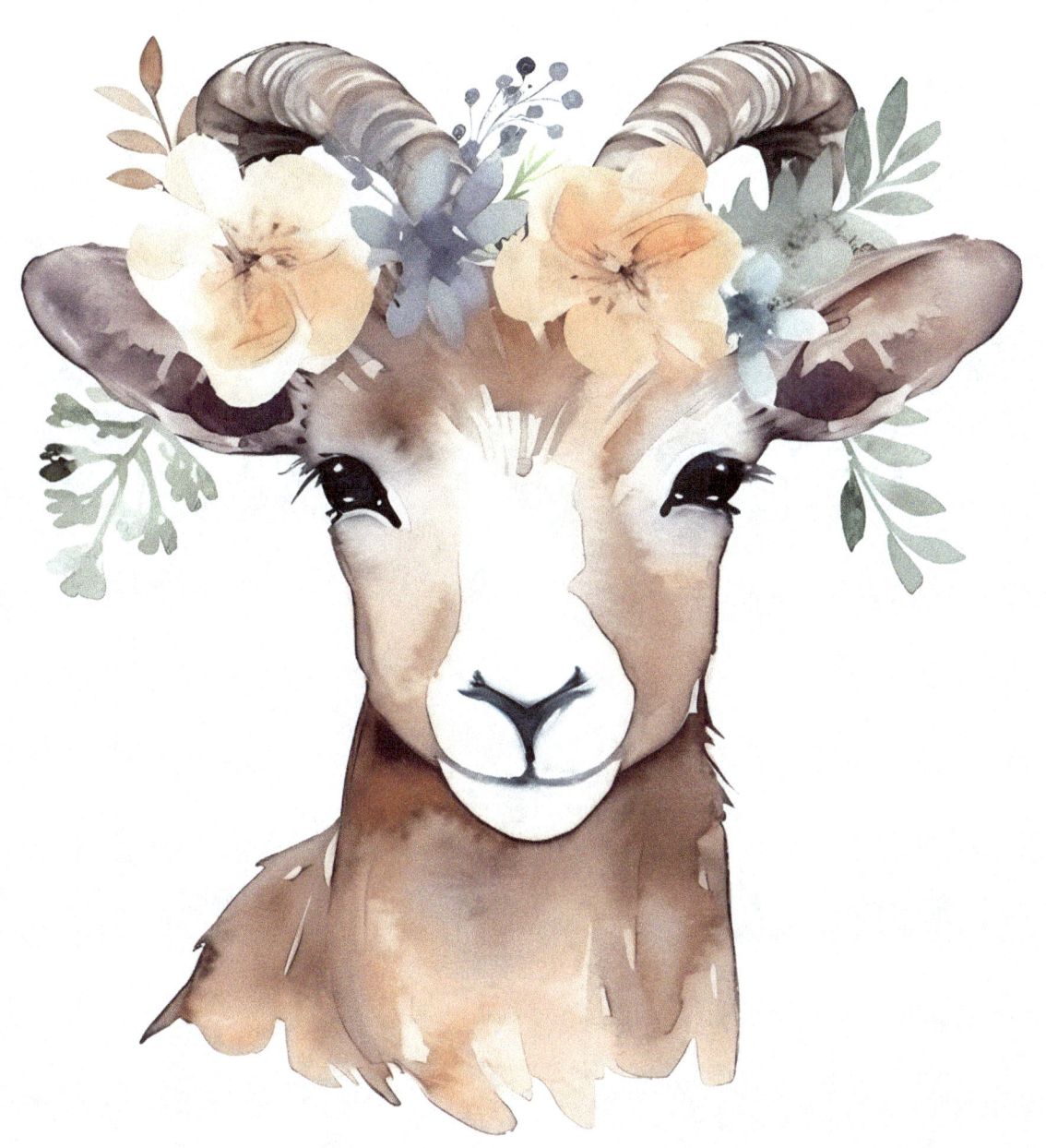

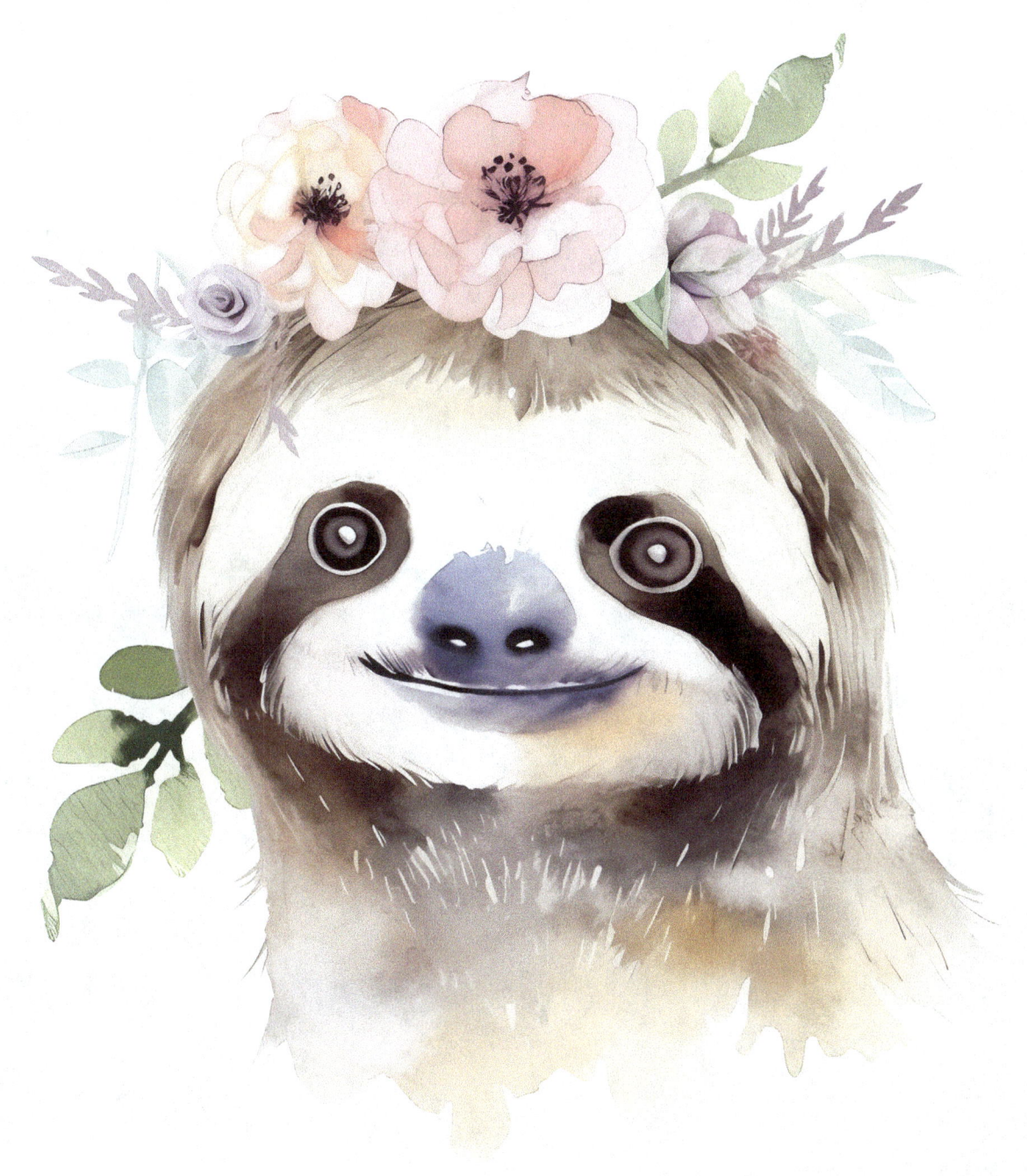

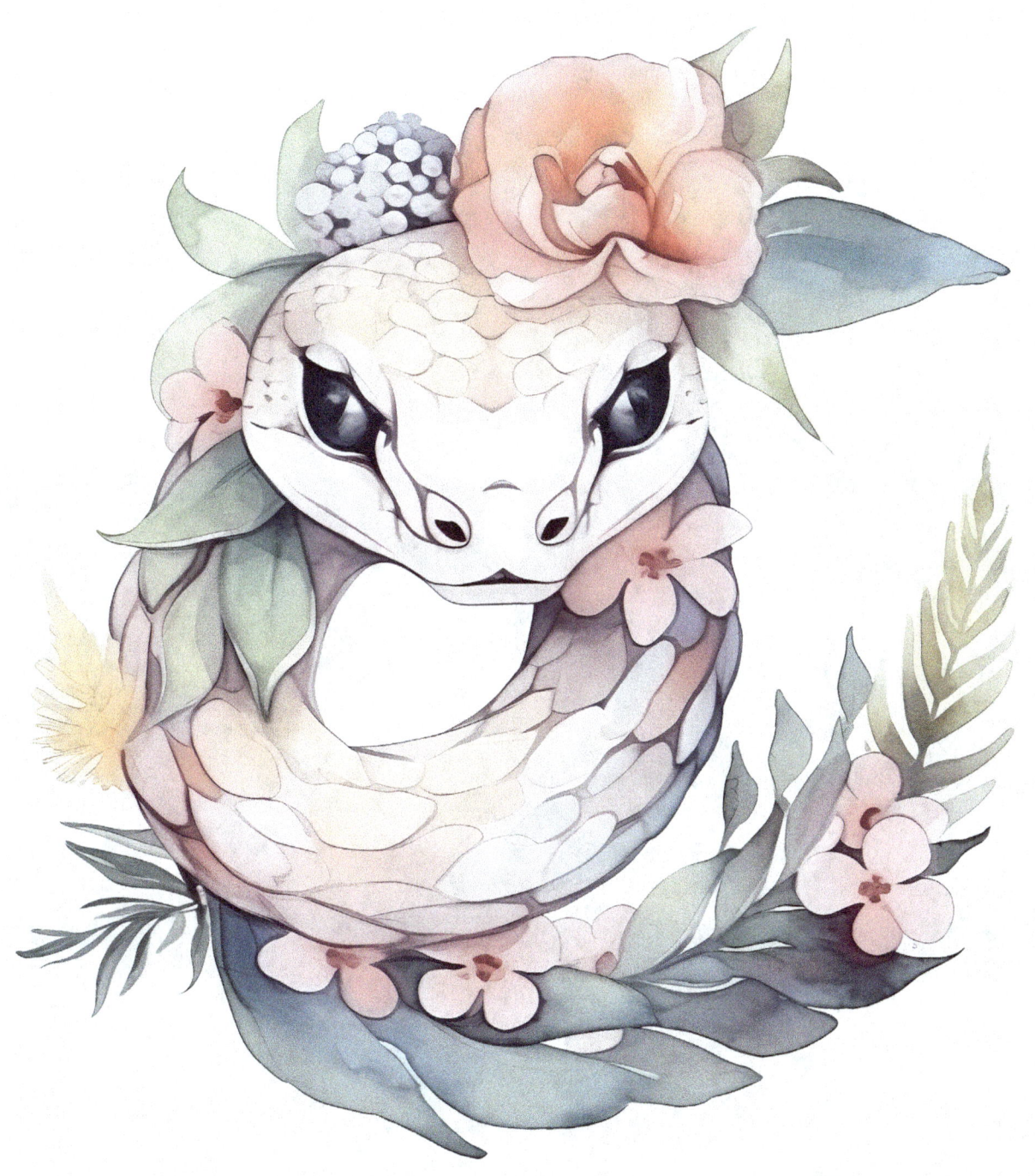

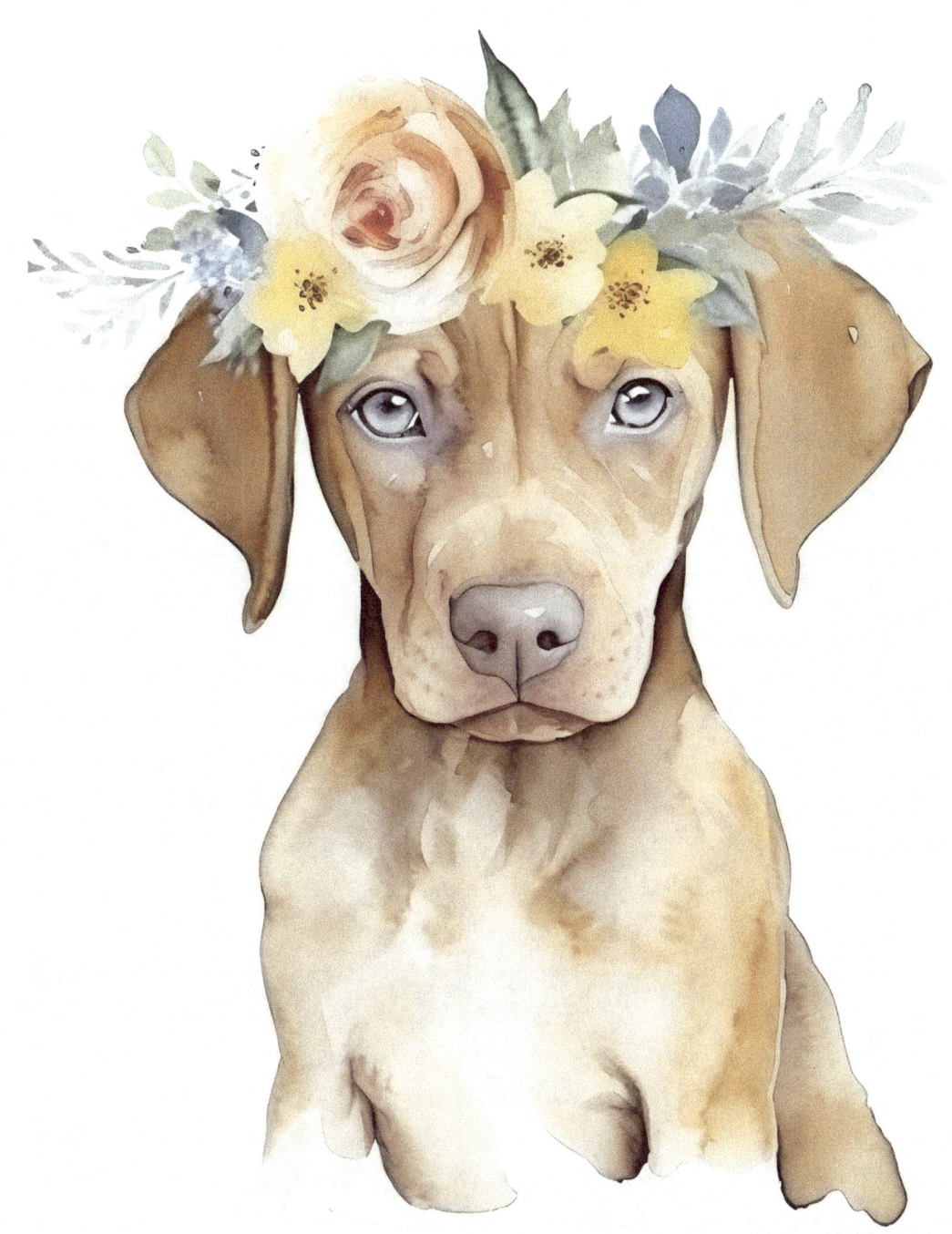

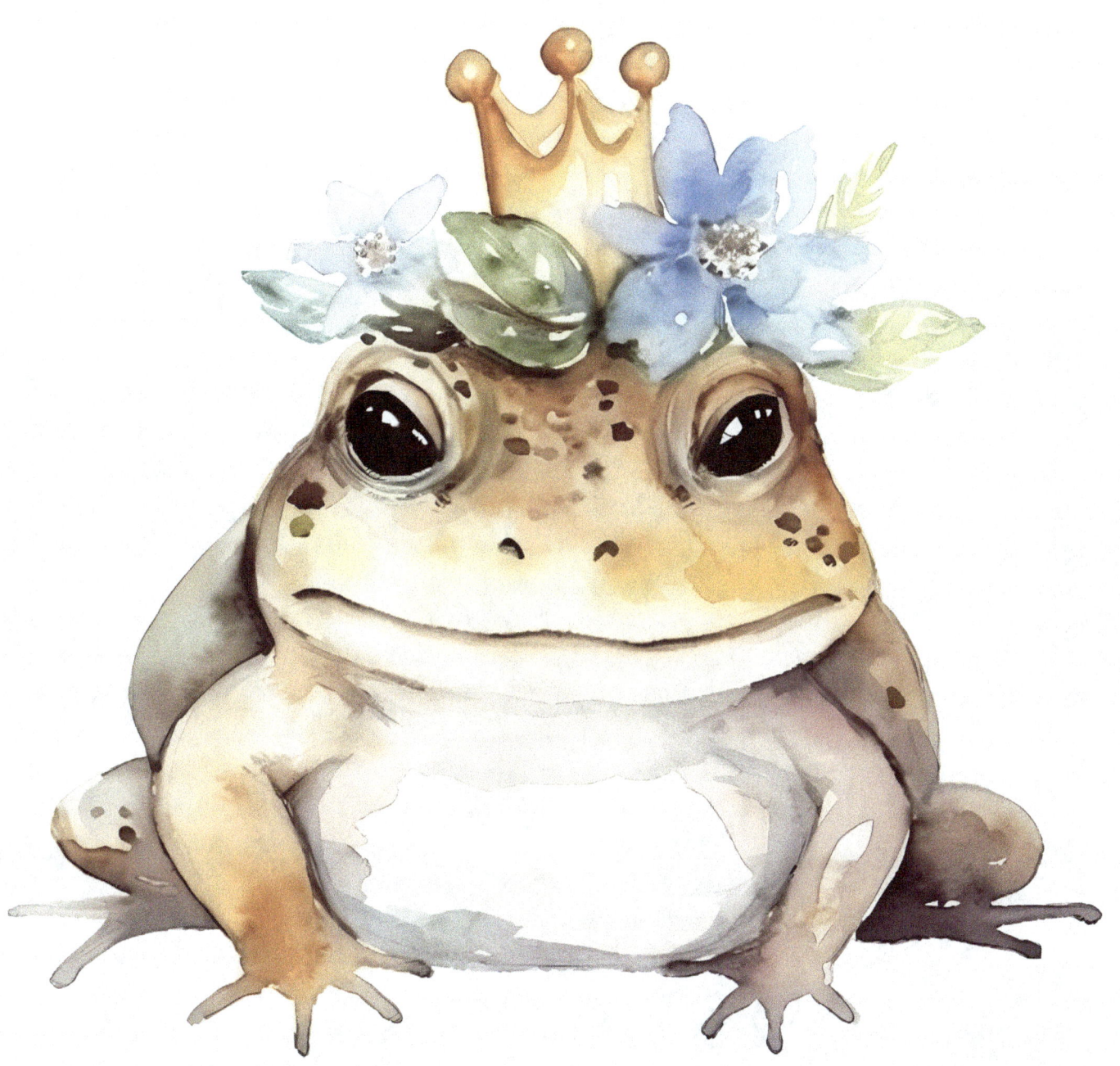

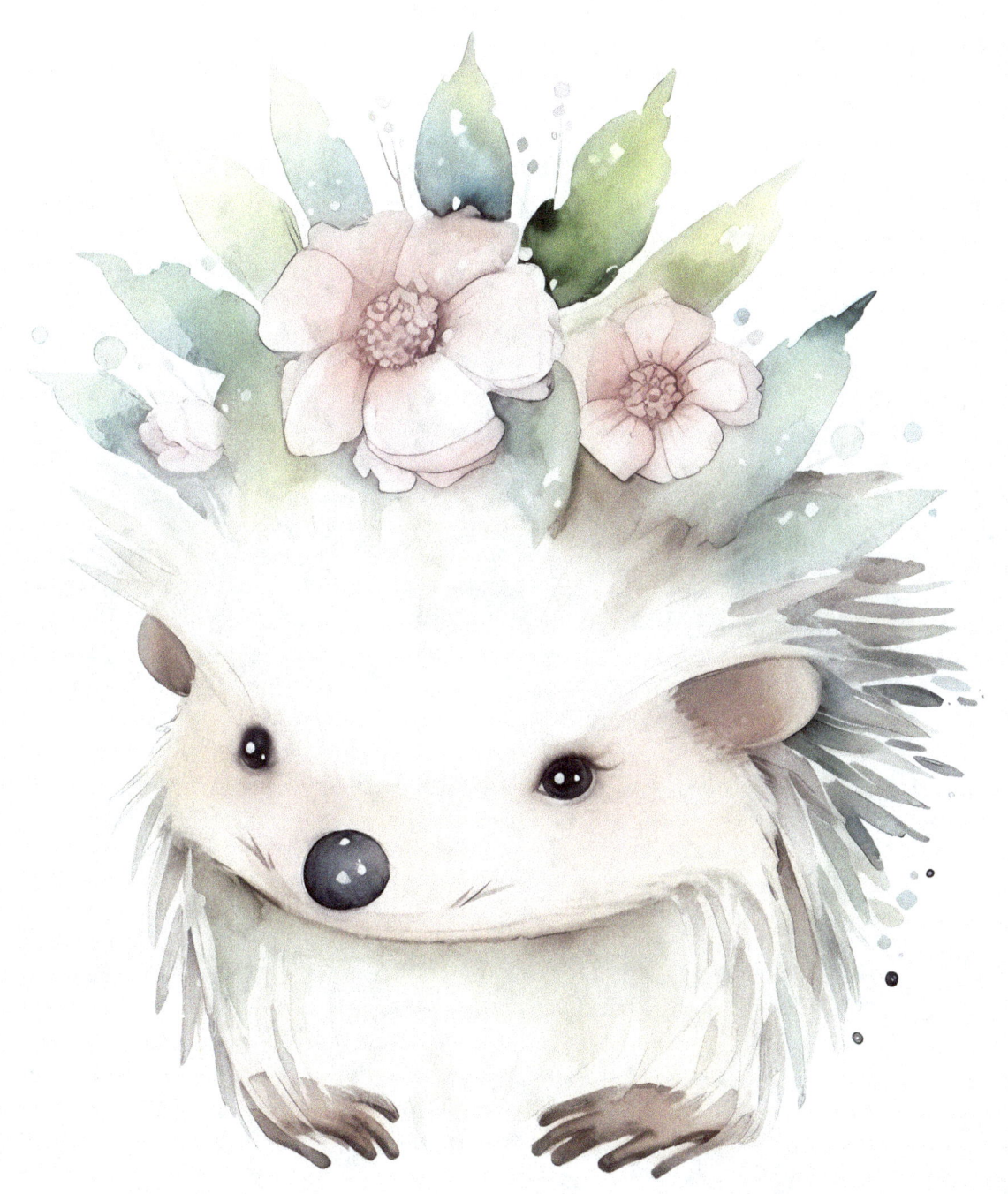

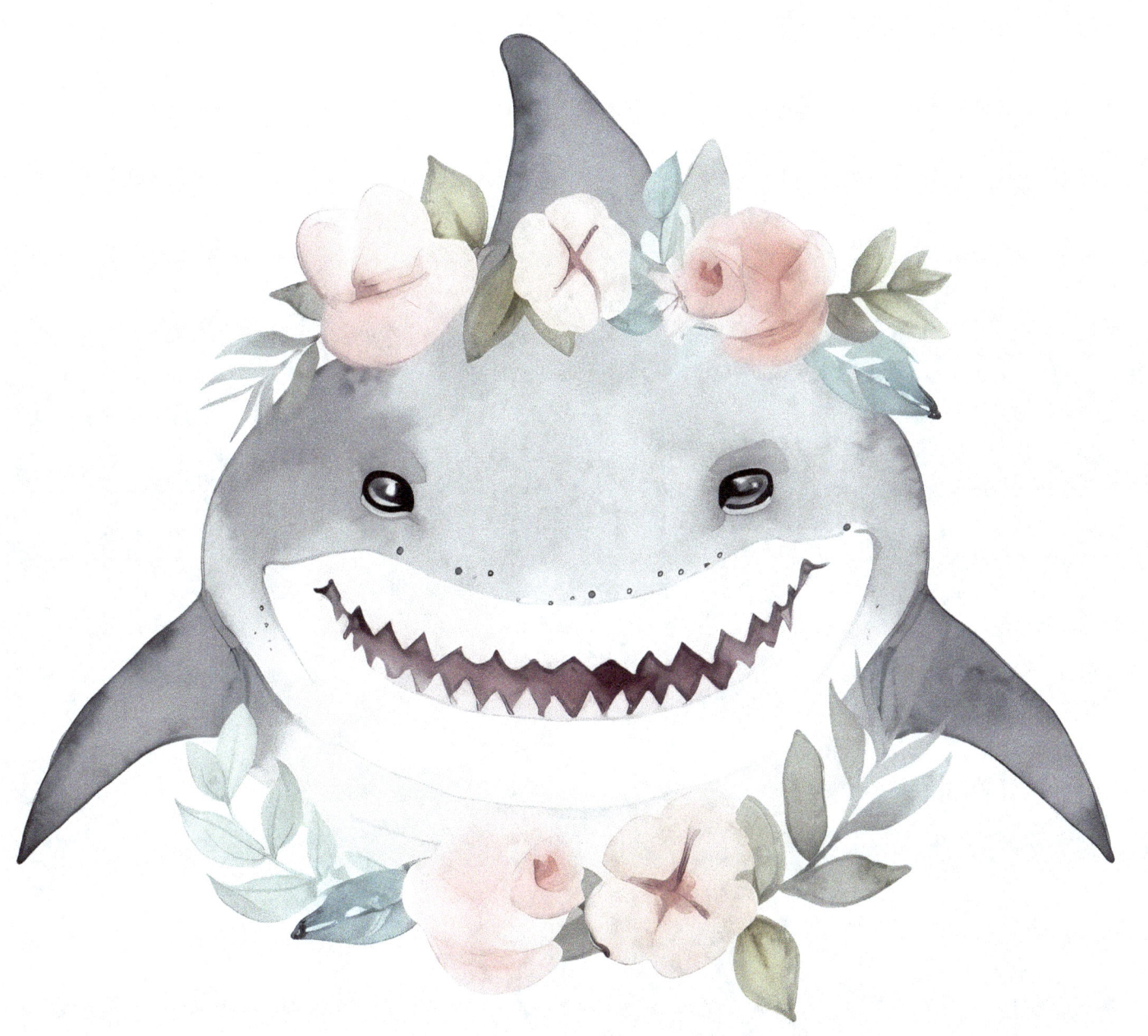

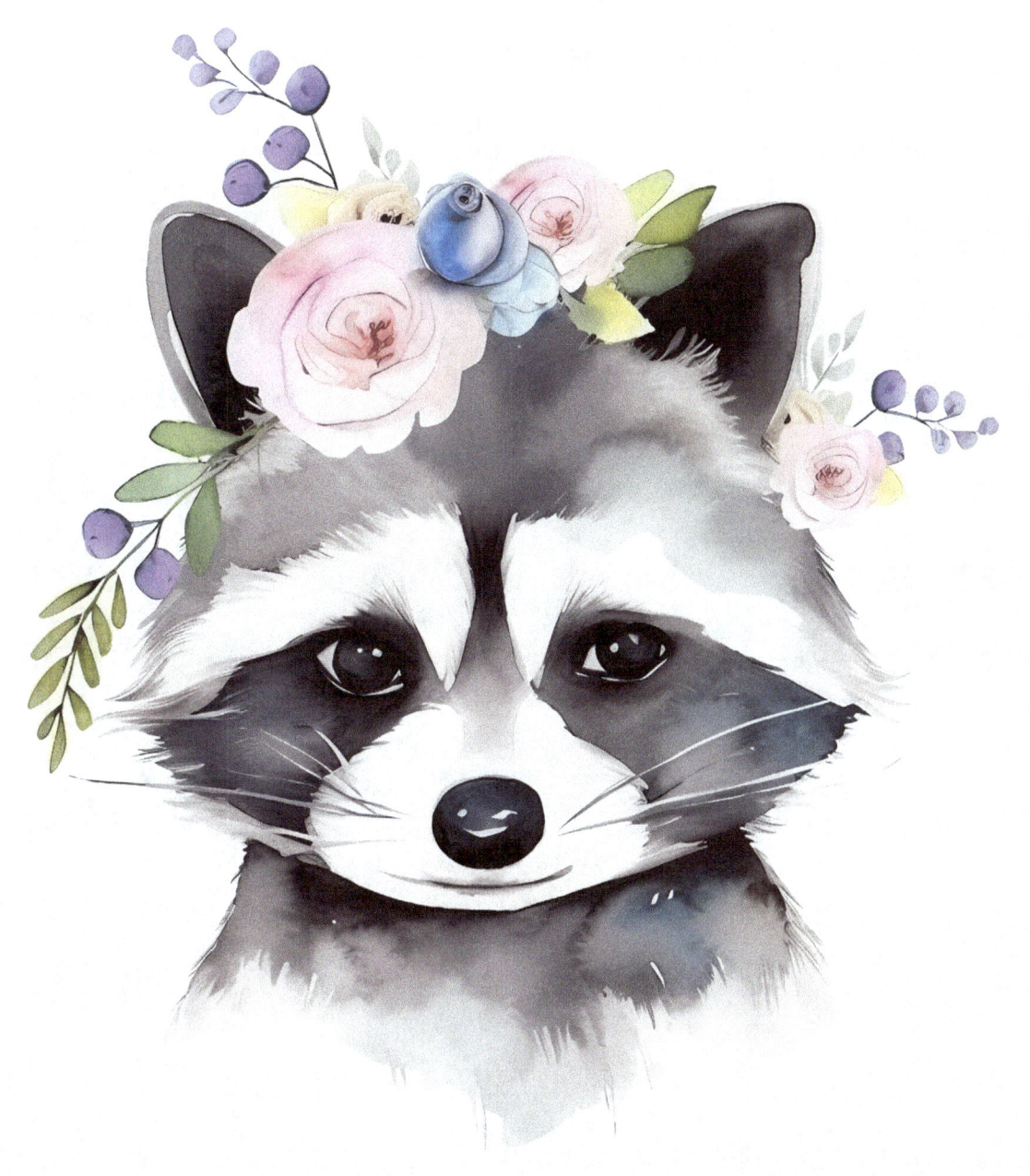

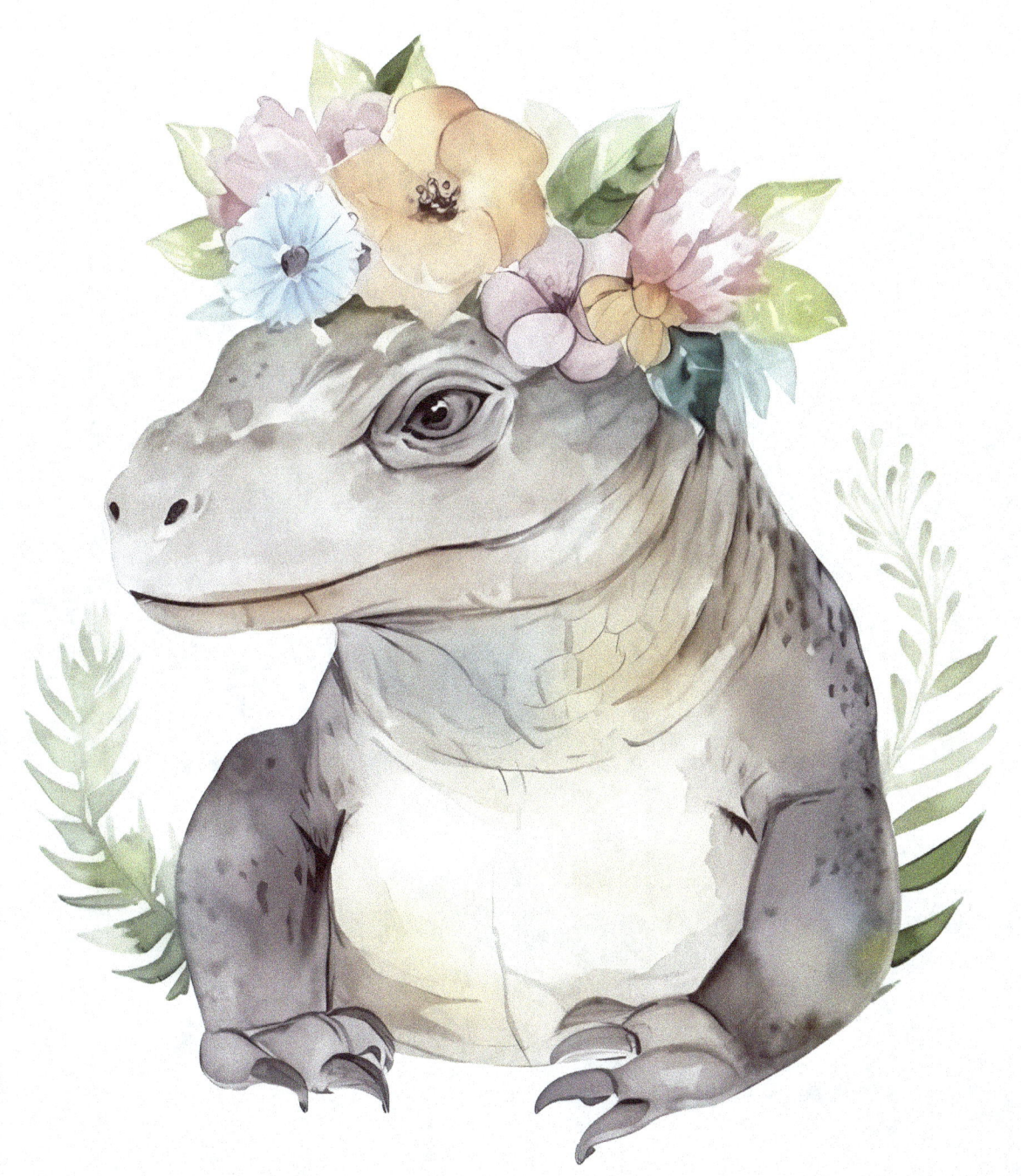

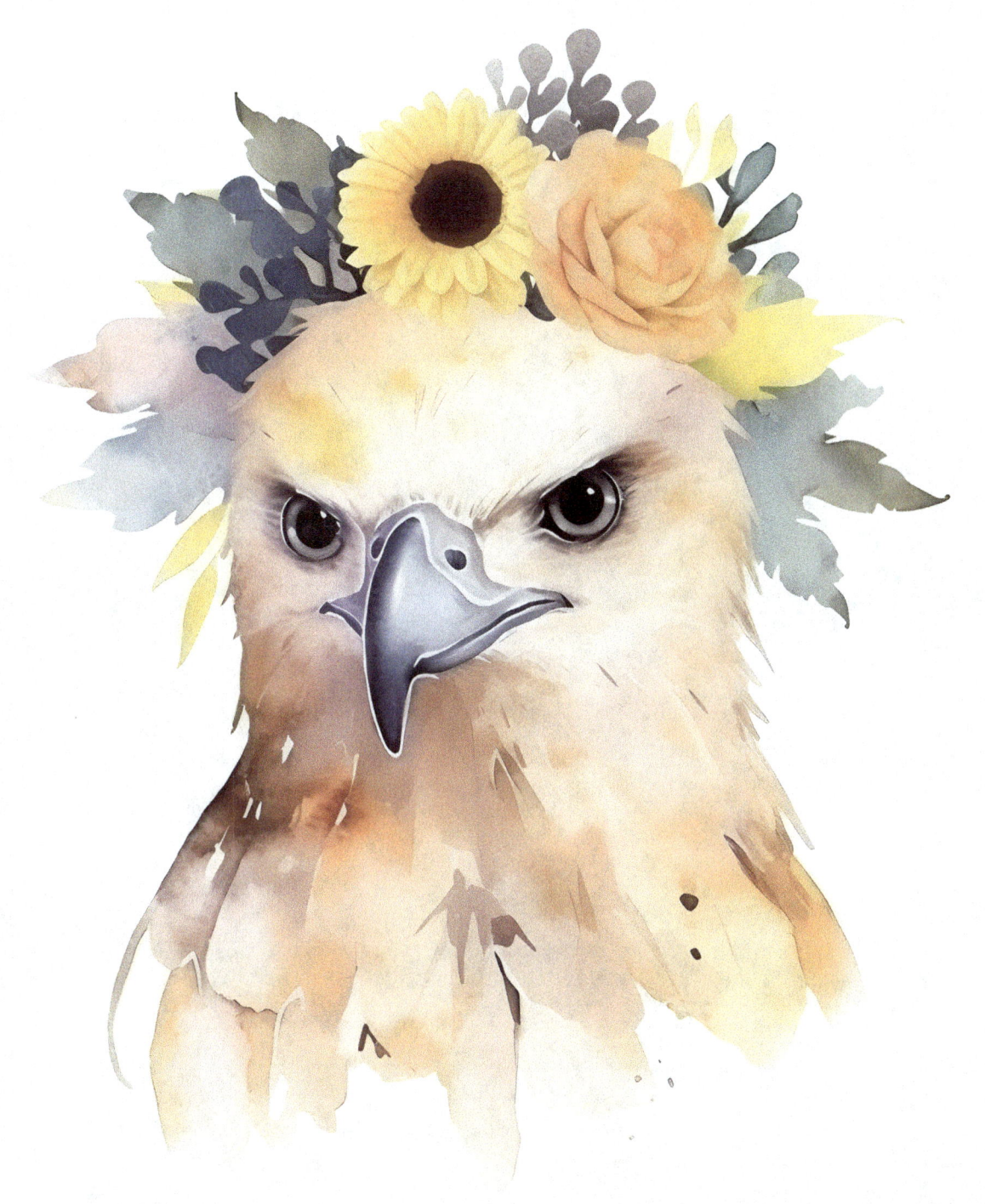

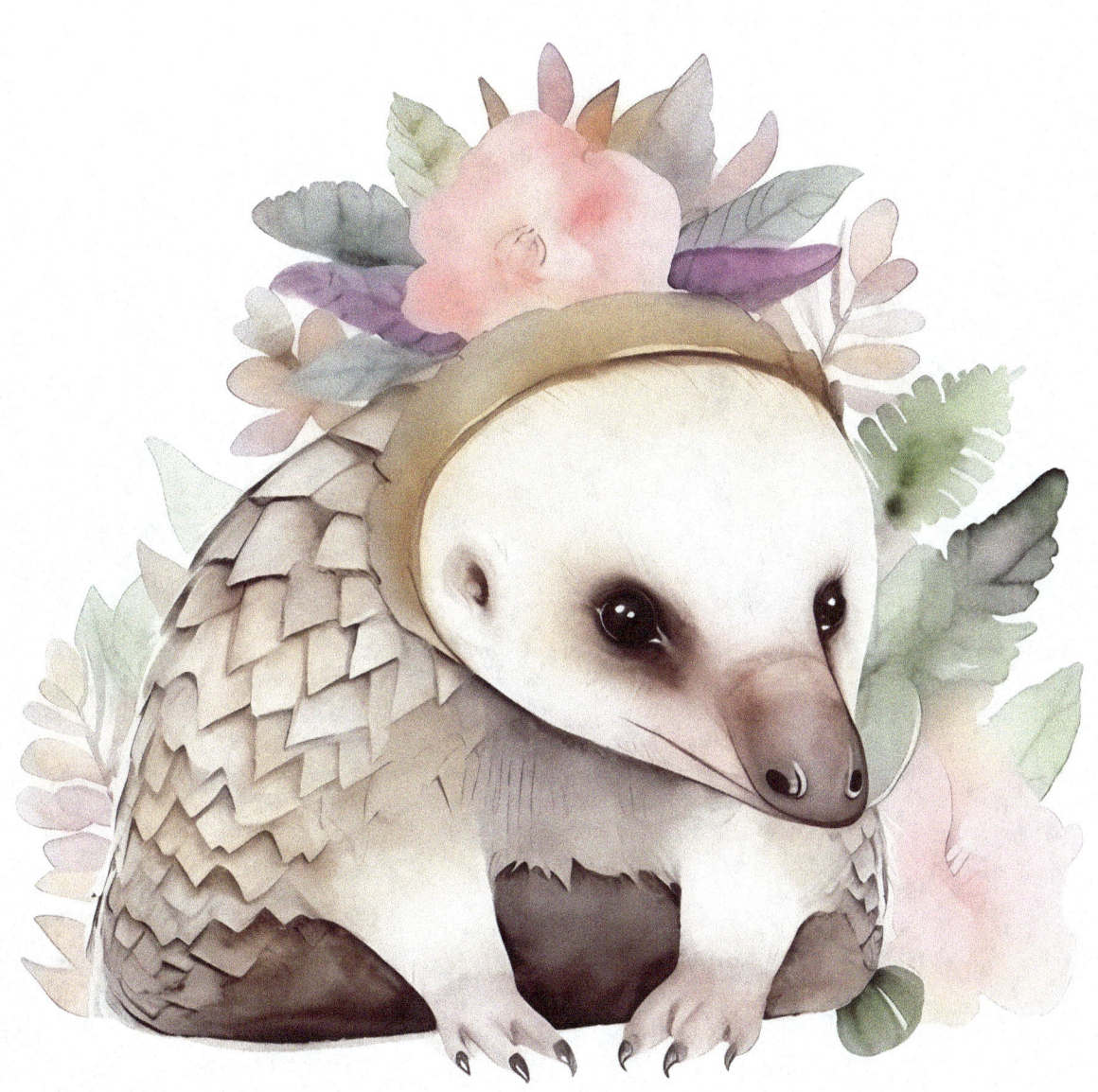

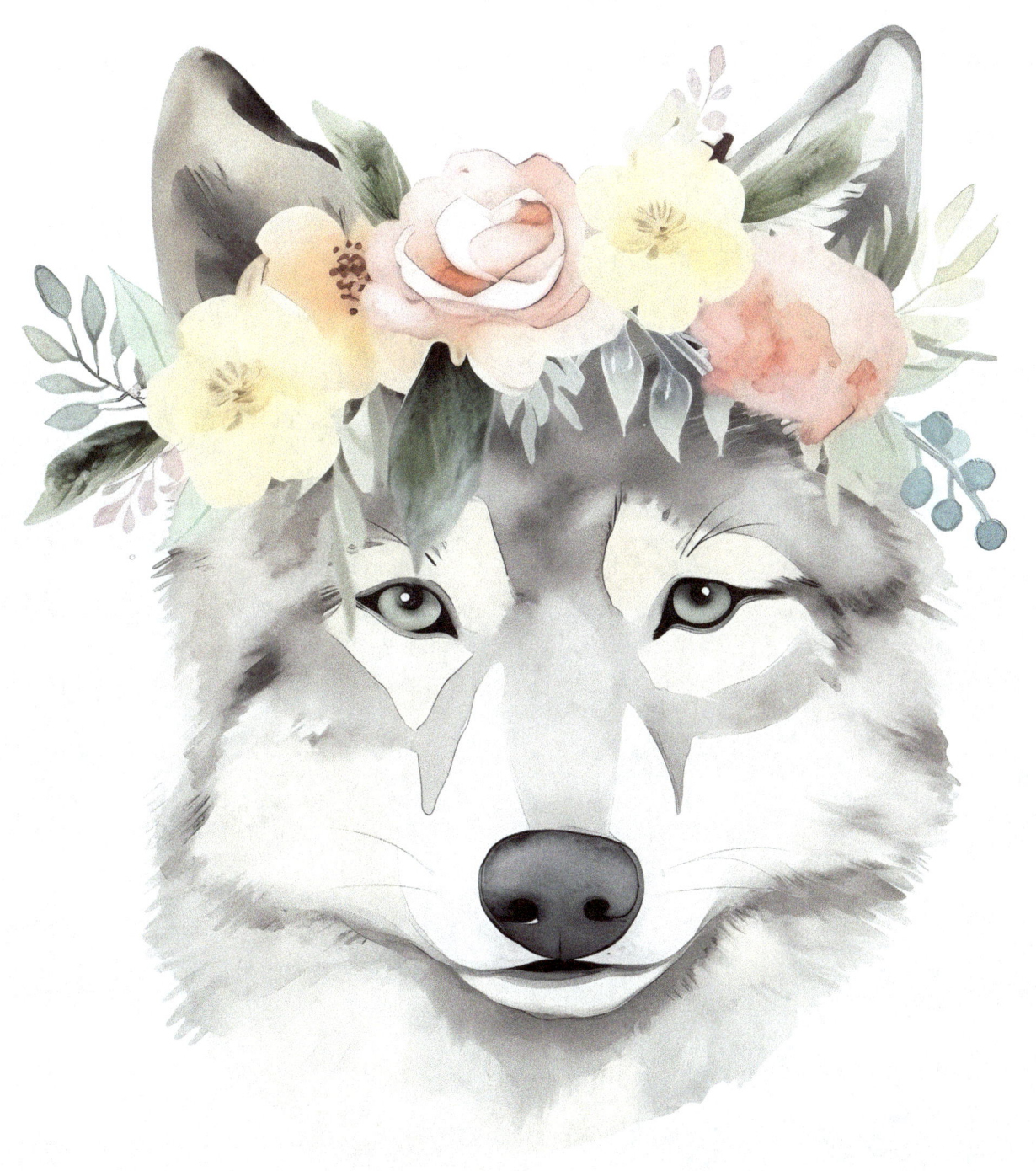

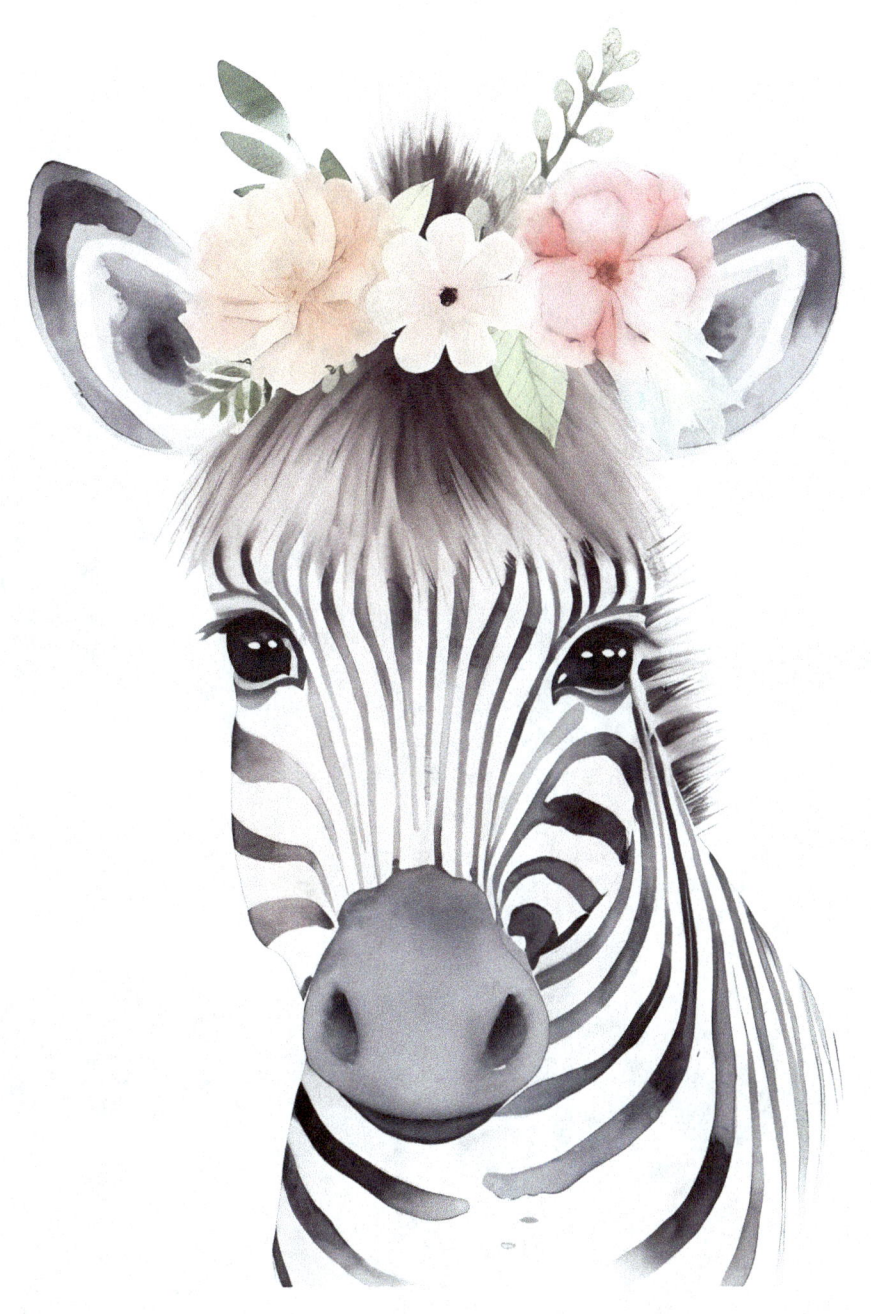

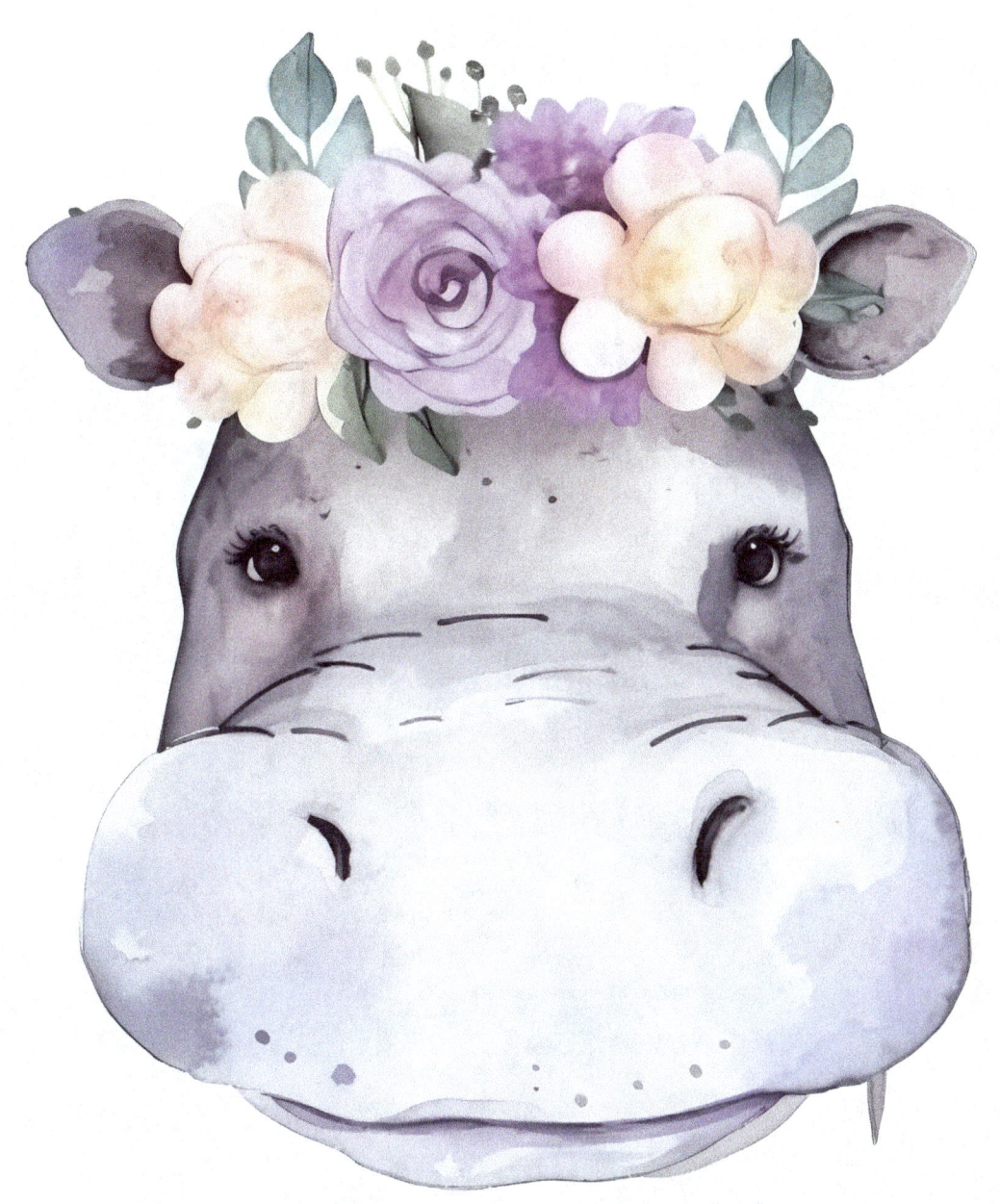

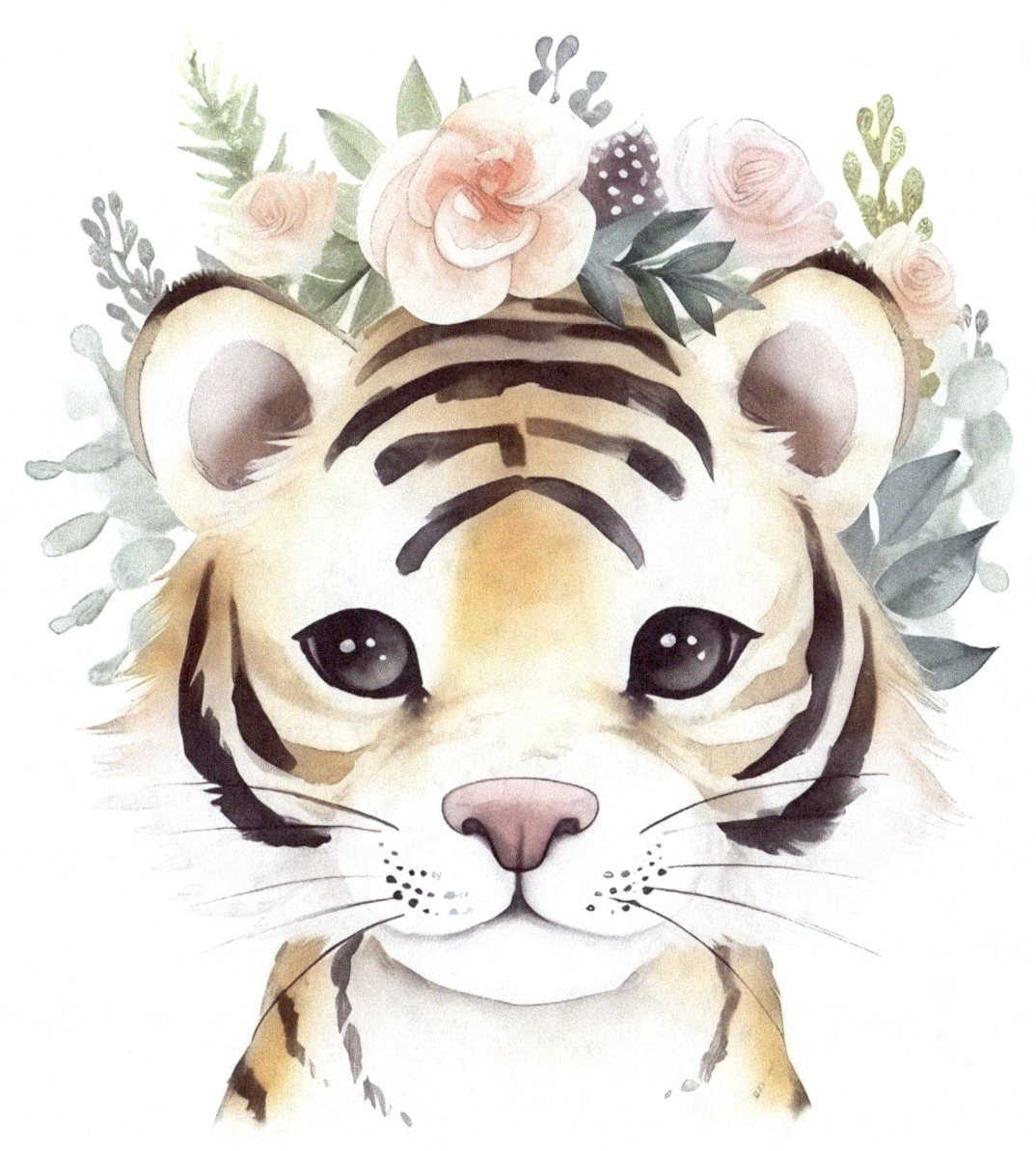

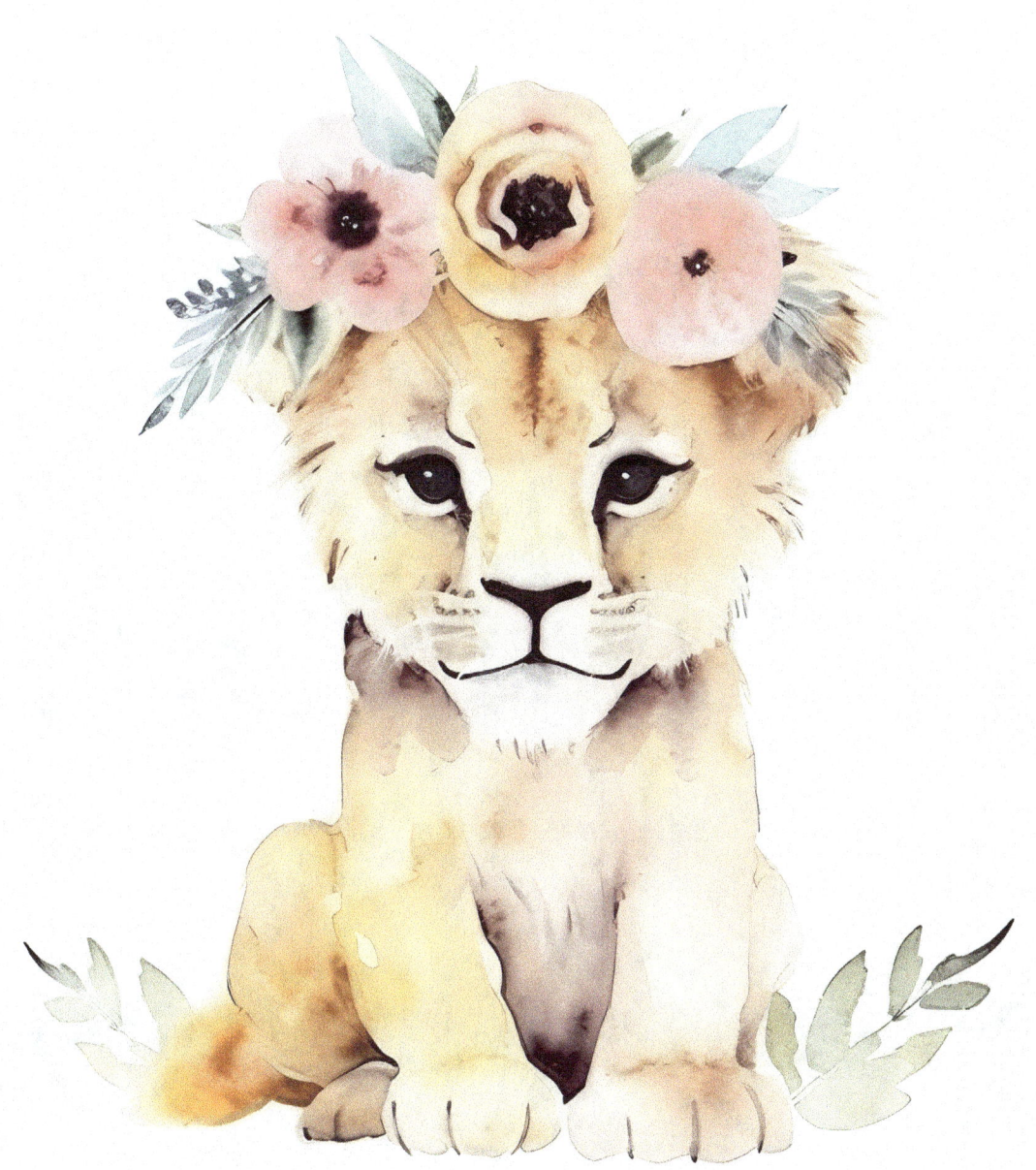

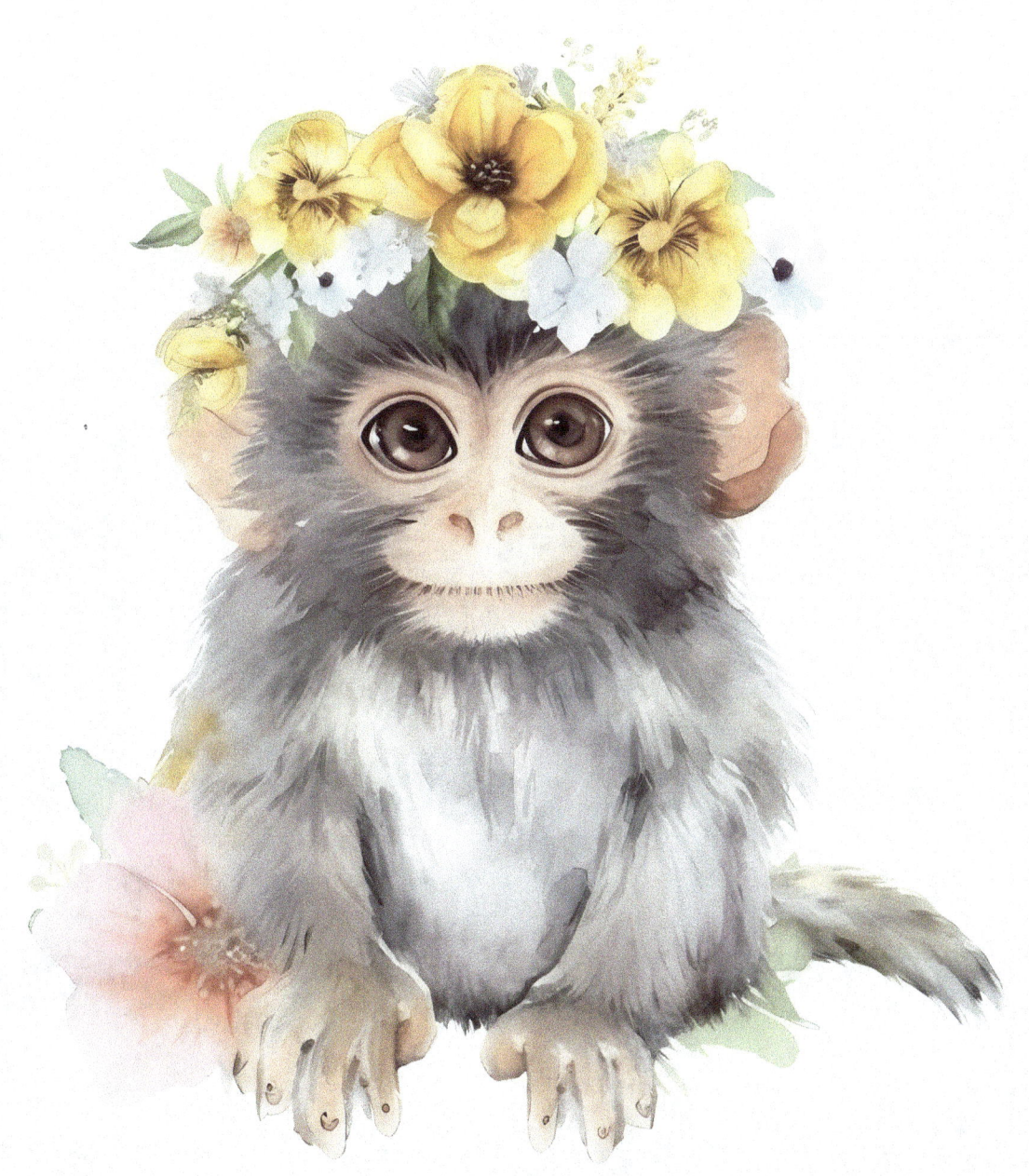

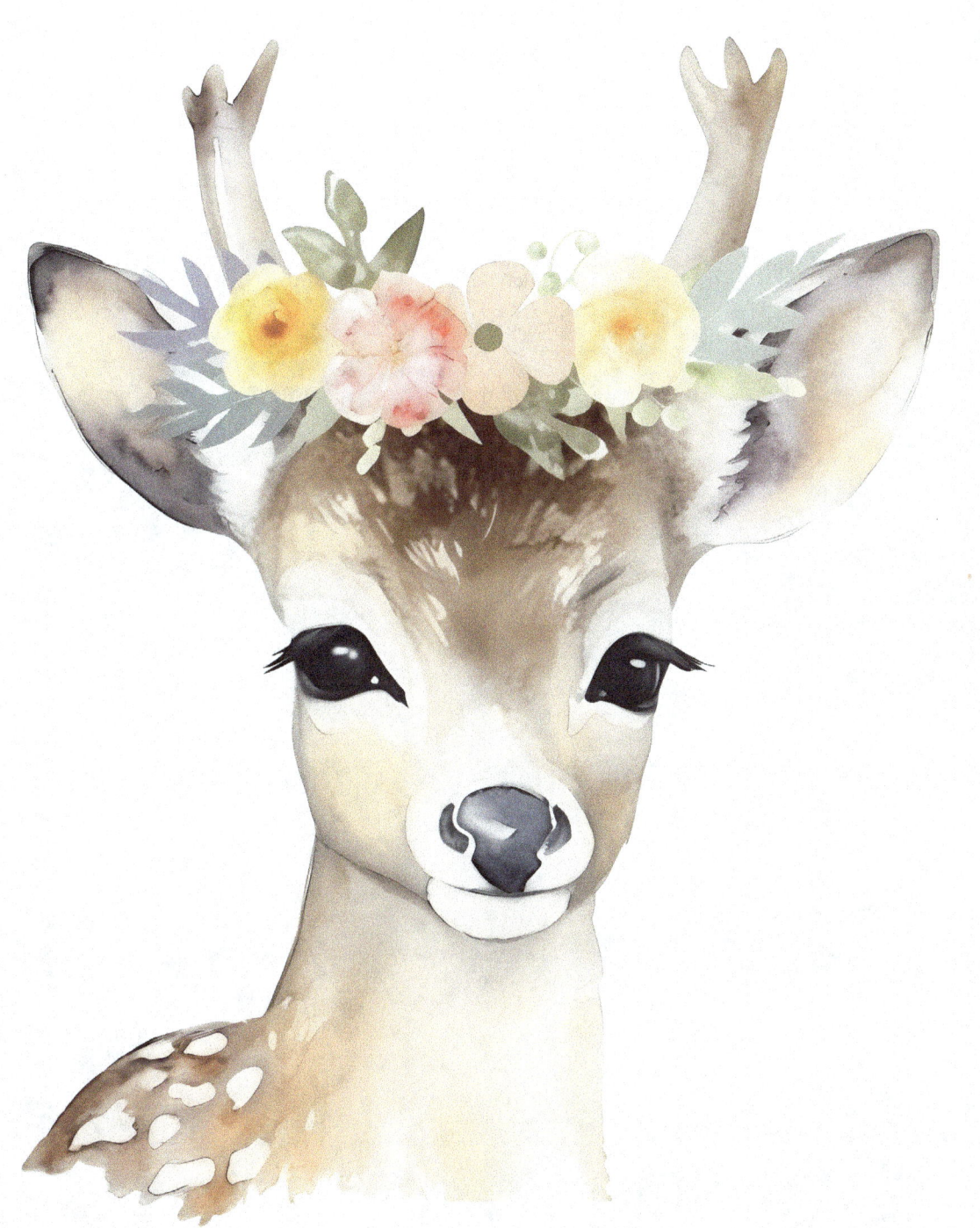

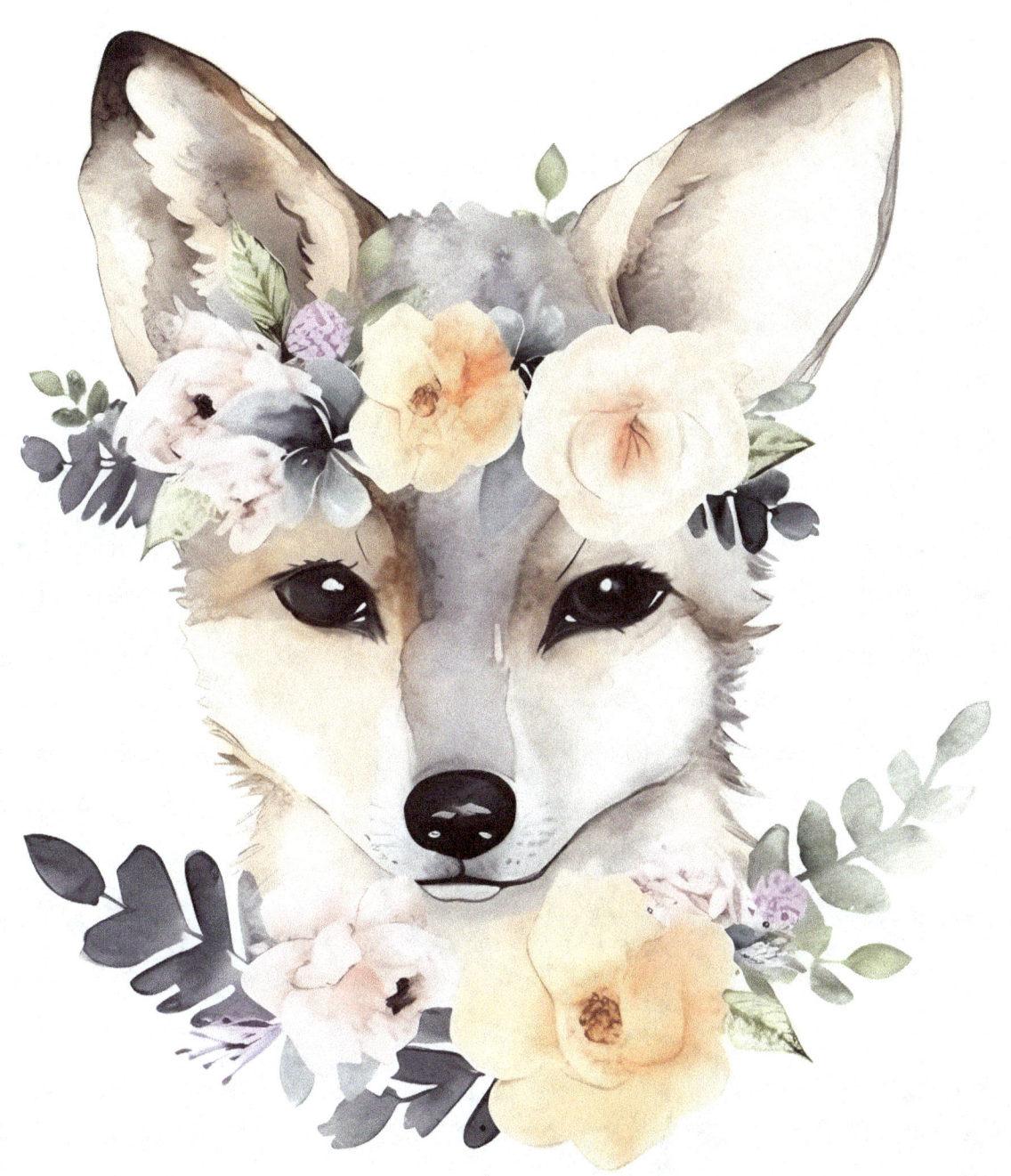

www.ingramcontent.com/pod-product-compliance
Lightning Source LLC
Chambersburg PA
CBHW081523220526
45467CB00010B/3023